¹99

Please your guests

A business guide

for small hotels, B&Bs,
guesthouses & farmhouses

Roy Hayter & Annette Allmark

MACMILLAN

HOSPITALITY *training* HtF FOUNDATION

First published 1998 by
MACMILLAN PRESS LTD
Houndmills, Basingstoke, Hampshire RG21 6XS
and London
Companies and representatives
throughout the world

in association with

HOSPITALITY TRAINING FOUNDATION
International House, High Street,
Ealing, London W5 5DB

ISBN 0–333–75113–2

A catalogue record for this book is available from
the British Library.

This book is printed on paper suitable for
recycling and made from fully managed and
sustained forest sources.

10 9 8 7 6 5 4 3 2 1
07 06 05 04 03 02 01 00 99 98

Design, typesetting and graphics by
Lloyds Publishing & Training, Llanidloes, Powys

Illustrations by Gallery, Soho, London

Printed in Great Britain by
Antony Rowe Ltd, Chippenham, Wiltshire

Acknowledgements

Critical Skills Working Party

Hugh Becker (Chairman), The Norman
Richardson House Trust

Rose Alderman, Milton Keynes College

James Brown, Academy of Food & Wine
Service

Catriona Butcher, Tastes Catering, London

Atique Choudhury, Yum Yum Thai
Restaurants, London

Adrian Clark, The Tourism Society

Mary Curnock Cook, British Institute of
Innkeeping

Julian Demetriadi, Apostrophe

Hilary Fradera, West Herts College

Bill Fraser, Petty France Hotel

Rosemary Griggs, Department for Culture,
Media & Sport

Patricia Hartley, Progressive Training

Kurt Janson, English Tourist Board

Maria Kenyon, Department of Trade &
Industry

Penny Lasko, Department for Education &
Employment

Andrew Lockwood, Hotel & Catering
International Management Association/
University of Surrey

Anne Marie McDonald, Department for
Culture, Media & Sport

Dave Mills, The Packhorse, Frome

Robert Parsons, Reading College

Gerry Price, The Brickmakers Arms,
Windlesham (Hampshire Pubs)

Christine Ratcliffe, Westbourne House Hotel,
Sheffield

Peter Russum, E Russum & Sons Limited,
Rotherham

Terry Savage, Union of Shop, Distributive
and Allied Traders

Charlotte Shepheard, Macmillan Press

Jim Watson, Licensed Victuallers Association

Joyce Willoughby, Charlie's Fish & Chip
Shops, Amble

and special thanks to

Caterer & Hotelkeeper, Food Service Management
and *Hotel & Restaurant Magazine* for
permission to draw on published articles.

Please your guests

Contents

Foreword

Guests are the lifeblood of your business and central to your life. In simple terms, more guests mean more profit. That is the first aim of this book: to help your business success.

Pleasing guests has other rewards, of course. Contented guests are easier and certainly more pleasurable to deal with than the dissatisfied. Guests who enjoy staying with you are those who return, and recommend your place to others. Possibly some of these guests become your friends. You have an enjoyable, satisfying way of life. That is the book's second aim: to help you get more personal satisfaction from what you do.

How to please guests may come easily or not. But no matter how talented you are in this respect, there are the times when you know you could have done better. Looking back, you realise you were ill-prepared, inexperienced, over-hasty, over-cautious, too trusting, too focused on what was convenient for you or your staff. There are the times when you just wish you had some guide on how to approach the particular situation. This is the book's third aim: to prepare you better for such situations.

Approach the book in whatever way suits you. Dip into the parts that deal with important issues of the moment. Look for the checklists that are relevant to a particular situation. Use the index to locate advice on specific problems. Or read the book from beginning to end: it will not take long!

Please your guests is one of a series of business guides published by Macmillan Press in association with the Hospitality Training Foundation. It is the outcome of a major initiative to develop information resources focused on the small hospitality business, under the direction of the Critical Skills Critical Industry Working Party (for membership, see acknowledgements page). Much of this material is being distributed free – mainly through suppliers of goods and services. Other items, such as the skill checks, are modestly priced. For more details, see pages 59 and 60.

1 Why guests stay with you

Why do guests stay with you and not with someone else? For some it is your friendly welcome and excellent service. For some it is your location. For some it is the value for money you give. For some it is none of these things, but perhaps because they were booked by a travel agent, the tourist office, or a secretary. Maybe everywhere else was full?

The real quality experience for hotel guests, according to survey findings, comes from a feeling of being cared for, comfort (especially in the bedroom and bathroom), the atmosphere and ambience of the hotel, quality of decor and attention to detail.

A genuinely helpful attitude, when nothing is too much trouble, is one of the criteria inspectors look for to distinguish excellence in guesthouses, inns, farmhouses and B&Bs. A warm, cheerful welcome, and guests made to feel at home are others.

Get to know your market

Understand the reasons why guests choose your place to stay, and you can make informed decisions on how to:

- design and provide what people want

- distinguish your product as better than competing ones

- attract those who want your product

- provide the 'during' and 'after-sales' service which will ensure guest satisfaction.

Personal service

In the hospitality business, the product has much to do with personal service. Your personality and the personalities of your staff contribute to this. As a small, independent operator, you have an

advantage over the large hotels, roadside lodges and budget inns: you can more easily provide for the needs of individual guests.

What guests want

Your own experience will tell you that there is no single or simple answer to what guests want. What matters a great deal to one person can be of little or no importance to another. Yet it is possible to identify what will please most people most of the time. According to national surveys, the top requirements of guests are:

- quality of service – favourite words are 'friendly', 'efficient' and 'attentive'

- cleanliness – the absence of anything which suggests poor hygiene

- facilities – basic comfort is essential, thereafter expectations depend on the price and what guests are used to.

What inspectors look for

The inspection criteria of the tourist boards and motoring organisations are another useful measure of what guests want. The checklist on the following pages focuses on the requirements for one to three stars.

Some criteria may not be appropriate to you, because your standards are higher, or the prices you charge restrict what you can offer. Nevertheless, going through the process will help identify where you can offer a better service, or upgrade.

What do your guests expect?

This checklist – based on the AA/RAC for one to three star hotels – is selective, to help you identify those improvements you can make without major investment.

GUEST CARE
- ❑ guests greeted and acknowledged in a friendly, efficient and courteous manner
- ❑ enquiries, requests, reservations, correspondence and complaints dealt with promptly
- ❑ management and staff well informed about facilities, local attractions and events

RECEPTION
- ❑ management/staff available to receive guests during day and evening
- ❑ guests directed to their room or provided with clear signage
- ❑ once registered, guests have access at all times (using front door key or security code if appropriate)
- ❑ payphone (unless direct dial in-room facilities available)
- ❑ assistance with luggage available on request

SAFETY & SECURITY
- ❑ information on procedures in case of emergency
- ❑ multilingual emergency notices or use of symbols/diagrams
- ❑ printed instructions for summoning assistance during an emergency at night
- ❑ means of securing bedroom doors from inside and out
- ❑ proprietor and/or staff on site and on call 24 hours a day
- ❑ adequate lighting for safety and comfort in all public areas
- ❑ sufficient light on stairways and landings at night
- ❑ car parking, where provided, adequately lit
- ❑ particular attention given to safety and security of guests in ground floor bedrooms

RESERVATIONS/PAYMENT
- ❑ bookings handled in friendly, courteous manner
- ❑ name, address and/or contact telephone number recorded at time of booking
- ❑ details of payment due provided, and receipt on request
- ❑ purchases clearly detailed on bill

GUEST INFORMATION
- ❑ messages taken and delivered
- ❑ tourist, travel and/or local information available
- ❑ early morning calls on request (or alarm clocks in bedrooms)
- ❑ shoe cleaning facilities
- ❑ iron and ironing board available

GUESTS TOLD ABOUT
- ❑ what is/is not included in the prices quoted, cancellation policy
- ❑ opening times
- ❑ major refurbishment work in progress, planned functions/events/bookings likely to inconvenience other guests
- ❑ house policies (e.g. no smoking)

REFRESHMENTS/FOOD
- ❑ hot and cold drinks available in public areas during day and evening
- ❑ food carefully prepared and presented and properly cooked
- ❑ at least one vegetarian option at each meal
- ❑ cooked and continental breakfast served for reasonable period
- ❑ arrangements for early departure include provision of some refreshments
- ❑ reasonable choice of substantial hot and cold dishes for dinner
- ❑ if set dinner menu, alternative dishes available on request
- ❑ snack and cold meal provision for late arrivals, by prior arrangement

HOUSEKEEPING
- ❑ rooms cleaned daily, look clean and smell fresh
- ❑ rooms checked daily to ensure high standard of cleanliness
- ❑ all beds made daily
- ❑ clean bed linen, including duvet covers, for each new guest
- ❑ bed linen, including duvet covers, changed at least every 3 days for stayover guests
- ❑ in-room crockery and glassware washed hygienically
- ❑ good housekeeping practice followed
- ❑ monitoring procedure for reporting broken or damaged items

More overleaf

BEDS

- ❏ in good condition, with sound base and sprung interior
- ❏ foam or similar quality modern comfortable mattress
- ❏ secure headboard or equivalent
- ❏ access from both sides of double bed
- ❏ minimum size of single beds: 190 x 90 cm (6'3" x 3')
- ❏ minimum size of double beds: 190 x 137 cm (6'3" x 4'6")

BEDDING

- ❏ 2 sheets, 2 blankets per bed + 3rd blanket, bedspread or equivalent
- ❏ two pillows per person in individual pillow cases
- ❏ duvets acceptable, provided traditional bedding available on request
- ❏ 100% man-made fibre sheets unacceptable
- ❏ mattress protector or under-blanket for each bed
- ❏ plastic or rubber mattress protectors not acceptable (except for a child's bed)
- ❏ spare blankets, pillows and non-allergenic pillows available on request
- ❏ no stained, torn or worn linen
- ❏ additional bedding in guest rooms wrapped

HEATING & LIGHTING

- ❏ fixed heating controllable by the guests
- ❏ entire bedroom can be heated adequately and quickly
- ❏ supplementary heating available on request
- ❏ no charge for heating
- ❏ bedside reading light for and controllable by each person, plus

light controlled from the door
- ❏ twin beds possibly sharing a bedside light
- ❏ overall lighting level at least 160 watts (single room), 220 watts (double room)
- ❏ shade or cover for all bulbs unless decorative

WINDOWS AND CURTAINS

- ❏ windows easy to open
- ❏ ground floor windows provide security when open
- ❏ opaque curtains, blinds or shutters on all bedroom, bathroom and toilet windows, including glass panels to doors, fanlights, and skylight windows
- ❏ ground floor windows have net curtain or blind

BEDROOM FURNITURE

- ❏ dressing table or flat surface of acceptable dimensions, convenient 13 amp power socket, adequate lighting
- ❏ mirror in which guests can see themselves from head to toe
- ❏ wardrobe or clothes hanging space, and adequate drawer or shelf space
- ❏ wire hangers not acceptable
- ❏ one chair in a single room, 2 chairs (or 1 chair and 1 stool) in twin/double

BEDROOM FACILITIES

- ❏ tea/coffee making facilities
- ❏ fresh milk available on request
- ❏ consumables kept wrapped or in lidded container
- ❏ guests do not have to operate kettle at floor level
- ❏ all available TV channels properly tuned in
- ❏ hair dryer advertised as available

on request
- ❏ waste paper container (non-flammable if smoking permitted)
- ❏ ashtray (if smoking permitted)
- ❏ drinking tumbler per guest (glass or scratchless plastic or wrapped disposable)
- ❏ sufficient, conveniently situated power sockets
- ❏ hotel services and facilities advertised in bedrooms
- ❏ 'Do Not Disturb' notice provided

BATHROOM FACILITIES

- ❏ bath or shower, washbasin and mirror
- ❏ adequate heating, covered light
- ❏ soap and soap dish, hook for clothes
- ❏ non-slip surface or mat for use in baths or showers
- ❏ mirror with good lighting, above or adjacent to wash basin
- ❏ convenient electric shaver point, indicating voltage
- ❏ hot water provided at all reasonable times
- ❏ fresh soap for each new letting
- ❏ clean hand and bath towels and bathmat provided for each new guest and changed daily (unless, as part of the hotel's environmental policy, guests are invited to and agree to a less frequent change of towels)
- ❏ lidded WC
- ❏ sanitary disposal bin
- ❏ toilet paper plus spare

Depends on grading

One star
- ❏ very informal, but competent service
- ❏ a designated eating area (e.g. bar) open for dinner, last orders no earlier than 6.30pm
- ❏ presentable mode of dress for management/staff, but may be casual
- ❏ functional but practical furnishings, fittings and decor in bedrooms, colour TV (unless in lounge), radio if no TV

Two stars
- ❏ quite informal service
- ❏ last orders for dinner no earlier than 7pm
- ❏ smart and professionally presented management/staff
- ❏ evidence of co-ordinated furnishings, fabric and decor in bedrooms, curtains lined, dressing/writing table and luggage stand provided, chairs upholstered on seat and back, colour TV, radio available on request

Three stars
- ❏ more formal service, with higher staffing levels, dedicated receptionist on duty
- ❏ last orders for dinner no earlier than 8pm
- ❏ staff usually uniformed
- ❏ bedroom furnishings, fittings and decor generally matched and well co-ordinated, colour TV with remote control, radio, direct dial telephone, hair dryer

Get to know your guests

You want your guests to be well satisfied and return – the majority of them, anyway! To be successful in this goal, you should get to know and systematically record the information which will help you to better provide for your guests' needs.

1 How the guest found out about you

This can form the basis for business decisions, confirm hunches, provide a different insight, even surprise you:

- advertisements, special promotions and paid-for entries in guide books: are they worth the cost, have you got the wording, size and design right?

- how much business you get from your tourist board, tourist information centres, and belonging to a hotel or guesthouse consortium: is the annual fee/commission justified?

- names of past guests who have recommended you: for a special thank you on next year's Christmas card

- how the chance guest found you: recommendation by someone in the town (do locals regard you as being cheap/expensive?), from your signs or advert in a local shop (are they eye-catching?), going past the building (what impression does it give?)

2 What the guest has come for or to do

For many of your guests, the reason for their visit is probably the same: on business (in a city or town hotel), on holiday (in a country or seaside hotel). You are likely to have available much of the information these guests need, and your staff can readily deal with questions and requests for assistance.

Nevertheless, it pays to look out for variations within your main market groups, and other significant reasons for staying, such as:

- business people coming to visit a new development or new business/factory: how can you attract other, similar, guests?

- contract workers laying a new pipeline: how long is the work going on for, will you have others staying?

- the closing of a local business: what impact will that have on your trade?

- followers of a leisure activity: how can you attract other such enthusiasts?

Knowing that a guest has come to a wedding or funeral can prepare you and your staff. Will the wedding guests be back to change in the late morning, which means all the rooms must be cleaned before then? Those people for the funeral will not enjoy your usual jokes.

When you find out that guests have come to walk, fish, rally drive, hear music, visit country houses and art galleries, etc. you can make suggestions and provide information that will help them get more out of their activity.

3 What the guest has spent

This helps at a general level to remind yourself which guests chose expensive wines, had the best or cheapest room, stayed because of a special discount. Comments may be more meaningful than a listing of names and amounts.

A promotion, such as a discounted room price to readers of the March issue of *Steam Trains Gazette*, is probably only worthwhile if the guests it attracts spend well on food and drinks, or fill your rooms at a time which would otherwise be quiet. Actual figures are more useful in this sort of analysis than gut feeling.

Special prices or discounts for group bookings can be compared against the amount spent on food and drinks, etc.

4 Which room the guest occupied

This is helpful to know when you have a variety of rooms: the view, quietness, colour scheme, size, furnishings, on different floors, etc. Some regular guests develop an attachment to certain rooms. It may be because they have difficulty with a lot of stairs, and by being offered (or asking for) their 'usual' room on the first floor, do not have to admit to their mobility problem. Some couples prefer twin beds to a double bed, and it shows good customer care if you do not need to be reminded of this.

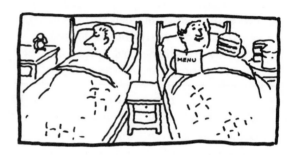

Knowing the type of room the guest had last time, may give you the opportunity to suggest a superior (and more expensive) room (on which you make more money): 'A standard single, as you had before, is available, or for only £4 extra I can offer you one of the new executive rooms.'

5 What special requests the guest has made

A request for a bed board, non-feather pillows, a non-smoking room, sheets and blankets in place of a duvet, *The New York Times* and an egg 'over-easy' each morning, would probably not have to be repeated on subsequent visits by the guest! Or would it?

Any one of these items is a typical example of the sort of request your returning guests should not have to make again. Of course, as the back problem may be cured, or reading habits changed, you should offer or confirm.

Even those requests of a one-off type, such as a fan on a very hot day can be usefully noted. For those times you are not available, you then have a useful memory aid to brief staff.

6 Personal details

Here is another area for using judgement. When a guest orders something special for a birthday celebration or wedding anniversary, and books to stay with you at the same period the following year, special greetings and a gesture such as flowers in the room, are going to be appreciated. But not if one of the anniversary couple is in the company of a different partner!

For guests you get to know well, a regular birthday card to their home shows you regard them as a friend as well as a source of business.

7 Contact details

These should be available from the reservation and/or registration record. Some guests will put only a street name and town in the registration book, and unwilling to make a fuss, you or your staff may let it go. However, incomplete details for a first-time guest mean you cannot put that person on your mailing list (if the guest is the sort you want to attract again). Nor can you return left property, or easily take action if the cheque bounces or the person leaves without paying.

Finding out this information

Much information about guests will come through natural points of contact:

- comments made by guests, and responses to what you have said – 'You look as though you might enjoy a nice pot of tea after your journey?' 'Yes please. We're en route to visit our elderly mother in south Devon, it's a treat to break the long drive'

- you observe guests, what they wear and do, their reactions – difficulty in walking, wearing a hearing aid, arriving with a rucksack and hiking shoes, a delighted expression when you say that breakfast is served until 10 am

WELCOME LORD AND LADY...

- questions asked without seeming intrusive – in conversation as you show a guest in business clothes with briefcase and portable computer to her room, 'Do you have an early start tomorrow, because if so we can bring a continental breakfast to your room?'

Be wary of the guests who do not like questions, answering with few words or a blunt 'No business of yours'. Switch to pleasant remarks about the weather or whatever to dispel any tension.

Recording the details

If you use a computer for reservations or accounts, create a database to record the information you have collected along with guests' names and addresses. On your registration form, give guests an option not to be put on your mailing list.

For the non-computerised, a card index system is practical and simple.

The blacklist

On to this will go the names of guests you do not want back, because they caused some problem. And if the booking has been taken before you discover the connection, at least you are forewarned. To cancel the booking might lead to action for breach of contract, or defamation of character if the person gets to know that he or she is on a blacklist.

Get the name from the start

Find a way to get the caller's name before you say accommodation is available, e.g. 'One moment while I get the diary. Could I have your name, please... Right, Mr Taylor, that is a twin for July 2nd, let me see ...'

Then, having found the name Taylor on your blacklist, 'I'm just turning to the page now, where are you calling from, Mr Taylor?' (to check you have the correct Taylor) 'Here we are ... Oh dear, I am sorry, we are completely full.'

If the blacklisted guest asks if there is anywhere else you recommend, be vague: 'You could try Talking Yellow Pages'. In a small town, to suggest contacting the tourist information centre might backfire. What if they refer the booking back to you. Or they deduce that because you sent the enquiry to them, you are full that day.

There is a much more positive reason for getting names quickly. A quick reference to the guest's history card will remind you to ask if Mr Taylor would like his usual room, a bed board, *The New York Times*, etc.

When not to bother

There is a point at which it is not worthwhile keeping an individual guest record. Take into account the likelihood that particular guests will come back and what your guests expect.

Regular returners to a place providing personal attention clearly value that, and the more you give them the better for business.

2 Turn enquiries into business

An enquiry is your first point of contact with new guests, whether it be on the telephone, face-to-face, or in writing. For returning guests, and regulars, it is the chance to reinforce their impression of the personal service you offer, your memory for names, and for the likes and dislikes of your guests.

You don't know when you answer the telephone or door what is going to unfold in the next few moments, and what the consequences of the call will be. What you don't want is to look back and think 'If only I had said (or not said) that', 'I wish he/she hadn't caught me at such a bad time', or some such excuse.

At those moments when you are not at your best, pause for a few seconds between what you are doing and picking up the phone or opening the door. Use this time to compose yourself, put a smile on your face and in your voice.

Good impression on the telephone

Many service businesses have a standard for answering the telephone: within 5 rings, for example. This gets the message to staff that good customer service requires the phone to be answered promptly.

THAT'S NO GOOD, I'VE BEEN HOLDING ON FOR AGES – I'LL TRY THE NEXT PLACE THEN

You cannot be by the phone all day and night. Some people, familiar with the challenges of running a small hotel, may patiently let the phone ring, or be prepared to call back at other times. To catch those potential guests who are less understanding:

- plan staffing and your work so that someone is by the phone as much of the day as possible

- install extra phone points, e.g. in the kitchen, laundry room and anywhere else someone is likely to be

- buy or rent a cordless phone, and carry the handset about the building with you

- buy or rent an answering machine

- buy or rent a caller display phone or unit, which tells you the time, date and numbers of all recent callers.

A no-cost option (for BT subscribers) is to dial 1471 after you have been out of earshot of the telephone. If someone has been trying to get you, you can return the last call – unless the number has been withheld or is not available for some reason. But be prepared: if you get through to a large business or organisation, the switchboard operator is unlikely to know who was trying to make a hotel booking. The caller may not want it known that he or she has used a work phone for personal purposes!

Another problem is the busy phone. A poor impression is given to the caller who repeatedly gets the engaged tone:

- try to keep your calls short and business like, and ask other members of the household to do so – but if a guest is having a long conversation using the payphone attached to the same line, there is little you can do!

- consider installing a second line

- consider the use of BT's call waiting service: a discrete beep tells you another caller is on the line, and this caller gets the ringing tone followed by a message to say that you know there is a call waiting.

Modern technology has transformed the range of telephone services and equipment available, and lowered the cost. Keep up to date with what is available, and the current prices.

What people expect

- ☎ call answered quickly

- ☎ friendly but professional greeting, using hotel name

- ☎ no long wait while the reservations diary, a note pad or pen, etc. is found

- ☎ use of their name

- ☎ details correct first time, e.g. what is required, dates, price range

- ☎ options given where appropriate

- ☎ important details confirmed

- ☎ no hard sell

- ☎ important information explained, e.g. how to find hotel, price, meal arrangements

- ☎ not too long on telephone

- ☎ offer to call back if delay in collecting information

Good impression face-to-face

Do you ever provide inspiration for a cartoonist: damp hands and flour-covered apron because you were making pastry when the doorbell went? With everything you have to do to keep your business going, it is just not possible to look a million dollars one hundred percent of the time. But your appearance will contribute to the impression people get when they enquire at the door about accommodation, meals, etc.

Choose practical clothes for whatever you are doing, which convey the right impression to put potential guests at ease. Cyclists and ramblers don't expect you to look like a society fashion model. On the whole, business guests are more conservative.

First impression wrong!

You know how first impressions count. From the outside, this place had won me over even as we were parking. Inside it was a different story.

We waited to order drinks. Three ladies at the other end of the bar were asking about wedding reception facilities and the older member of staff was trying to answer their questions about menus, seating capacity and so on, while serving her own customers and looking after a young student who, it soon became apparent, was a new employee.

The lady behind the bar was having to take orders at tables as well. As we drunk our drinks, the couple whom, a few minutes earlier, she had waved over to "that table there", were asked to move: they were on the wrong table. As we finished our drinks, I heard the student being told "Try and spread the orders out, we've only got one chef tonight."

Reader Diaries, *Caterer & Hotelkeeper*. Graham Webb is manager of Towle's Country Restaurant, Hampshire

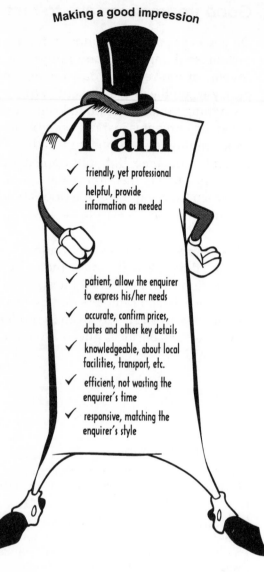

Making a good impression

I am

- ✓ friendly, yet professional
- ✓ helpful, provide information as needed

- ✓ patient, allow the enquirer to express his/her needs
- ✓ accurate, confirm prices, dates and other key details
- ✓ knowledgeable, about local facilities, transport, etc.
- ✓ efficient, not wasting the enquirer's time
- ✓ responsive, matching the enquirer's style

Good impression on paper

A friendly handwritten postcard or note accompanying the details the enquirer asked for, gives an impression of personal attention and informality. A brochure on its own suggests you cannot be bothered. If you find a typed or word-processed letter easier, keep away from old-fashioned expressions like 'your letter of 12 inst.', 'assuring you of our best attention at all times', 'I acknowledge your enquiry of ...'

Why the enquiry?

Look for clues, and ask questions so that you get and can give full information. Even the simple enquiry about prices or availability of rooms can disguise a wide range of circumstances, for example:

- enquiring on behalf of the boss: wants reassurance about your standards – here your rating by the tourist board/ guide books, acceptability of credit cards, availability of bar and restaurant means more than a warm welcome

- asking on behalf of a relative or friend – may be fussy and ask many questions, or the other extreme of not mentioning key information, e.g. that the friend smokes heavily (and all your rooms are non-smoking)

- someone with little experience of hotels – thinks £25 is for the week

- a group of people – your chance to quote a discount, or perhaps discourage the booking

- a hotel booking agency or travel agent – payment may take a long time and commission deducted

- a competitor – establishing what your prices are, perhaps how busy you are

- a company selling products or advertising – to gain your interest.

Often a regular guest enquiring by phone will not give a name: so do ask early in the conversation. Otherwise, if you have said you are fully booked as an excuse, e.g. because you wish to avoid those attending a rowdy local event, and then the enquirer says, 'Oh, it's Jim Smith here', you cannot rescue the situation.

What the enquirer is looking for?

Does the enquirer know what you offer, because of a recommendation, previous stay or other information, and simply require details of availability? Or is there some other need, which you have to find out more about to avoid disappointment: planning a celebration, looking for a particular atmosphere (log fires and oak beams), wanting to impress business associates, requiring somewhere low-cost, in search of peace and quiet, always takes the elderly dog, hates children?

What alternatives can you offer?

You do not have a single room available, but you can offer a very comfortable twin or double at a special price of £X for single occupancy. You are heavily booked on those days, would the previous or following week be possible? No family room, but you can put a fold-up bed in your double room.

What will secure the best deal?

High pressure selling may not be your style, but there is little to be gained by being too reserved or shy. Some people happily fall in with the suggestion that for a few pounds more they can have a four poster bed, or by paying for three nights they can have a fourth free. If you find the booking would be for all or most of your rooms, offer a discount to clinch the deal. If no breakfast is required, can you lower the price or provide a packed lunch?

Turn enquiries into business

The local network

Those casual conversations with suppliers, other local business people, neighbours, your staff, family and friends are opportunities to spread the word about the improved menu, extended opening season, refurbishment of the bedrooms. There are dangers, too. Amusing stories about guest behaviour turn into gossip: 'you can get up to anything you like in that place'. Bad news, you told someone of a minor water leak, gets distorted: 'they are closed for repairs'. Troublemakers have a field day: 'an ambulance was outside there the other day, the second guest to catch hepatitis' (yes, one of your guests was ill months ago, but in this case, the ambulance crew were staying).

Nuisance callers

To have someone trying to sell you something on the doorstep or by phone (those calls which ask if you are the proprietor or manager) can be annoying at the best of times, but in the middle of cooking or serving dinner, it's the limit! So are the faxes selling mobile phones or travel offers which wake you up in the middle of the night.

Be firm, yet polite to sales callers: 'thank you – but no thank you'. You never know when you may need to use their service or if they will one day use yours. Nor do you want them telling other people in the area how rude you have been. Delaying tactics will be seen through: 'I'm busy – call later' simply invites the sales person to make an appointment.

Phoney fax requests

Simon Haggarty, general manager of the Knoll House Hotel in Wiltshire became suspicious when it took six minutes to fax information on the hotel's tariff and facilities to a George Morris in Hong Kong. The incoming fax had taken 46 seconds to reach the hotel.

ICSTIS, the telephone standards body, after several other complaints about the number, which is an overseas premium rate service, has barred access to the line.

According to ICSTIS's code, faxes must carry contact details and pricing information and indicate when they are premium rate services. Anyone concerned about premium rate numbers can call the ICSTIS helpline on 0800 500212.

Caterer & Hotelkeeper

3 Take bookings the smart way

'Professional, but friendly', is the impression you want to leave guests with after they have made a booking. Efficiency matters because you must get certain information (name and contact details of the guest, type of room required, when the booking is for) and give certain information (the price, where to find your place). Friendliness is where you can respond on an individual basis to the guest, and convey the style of your hospitality.

If the reason for the visit is mentioned, or there is an opportunity in the conversation to find out why the guest is coming, you can give other, relevant, information, such as how to find out about walks in the area, local transport facilities and special events of interest.

Efficiency first

No matter how friendly you are, a booking error can do great harm. Remind yourself of what can go wrong, then consider how to avoid such situations.

Misunderstanding and/or lack of knowledge about hotel terms

Father and son arrive and you realise they must have wanted twin beds, not a 'double' as the father stated. You can usually tell when someone is not used to making hotel bookings. You could:

1 ask the name of the second guest

— if this embarrasses someone bringing his/her partner, you can quickly put this guest at ease by continuing in a friendly tone

— if you get 'Mrs Roberts, of course', you might reply, 'Thank you, sir, may I please have your wife's forename... and yours please...'

— a reply 'my son, John', would alert you to the misunderstanding, and you can confirm 'I have reserved a room with two twin beds, for you and John on the night of...'

2 confirm the bed arrangement

— by saying 'Thank you, Mrs Evans, we have booked a room with one double bed for two people for the nights of...'

An important detail is overlooked or got incorrect

Various couples have arrived the previous evening. Although they don't seem to know each other, you realise from the conversation over breakfast that at least three couples are here for a wedding in the afternoon. They have booked a two-night stay, so it makes sense. However, as 12 o'clock approaches, there is still no sign of a departure of the fourth couple, booked (according to your recollection) for one night only, and you have just heard that the guests booked into that room will be arriving at 1.30 pm. You have no other suitable rooms.

To avoid such a difficulty, you could:

1 follow a set routine to confirm all details for telephone bookings

— saying, for example 'Thank you Mr Stone, that is a room with one double bed at £45 for two people, including breakfast and VAT, for the one night of Friday 3rd of ...

2 ensure that length of stay is confirmed when guests register

— if you use a registration book, ask any guest who does not bother to complete this column 'You are booked for two nights, I believe, so the date of departure will be ...?'

3 confirm all bookings in writing

— although this takes time, it gives the opportunity to send your brochure, perhaps encouraging the guest to have dinner as well. However, the guest may not pay sufficient attention to your letter to notice the mistake, and to save face, might deny receiving confirmation.

4 both you and guest confirm in writing

— time consuming, and makes the booking process more difficult for your guest. If the guest's letter is ambiguous, e.g. 'to confirm my booking for a double room, arriving 5 June', then further correspondence may be necessary.

Get the right balance

Secretaries making a booking for their boss want efficient service. The call should not take long and any questions should reassure the secretary that you know how to deal with business people. 'Shall I reserve a table for dinner?' will do this. A long, rambling explanation about the need to book won't.

Be alert for, and respond quickly, to the person:

- who dislikes chat

- phoning from a call box, short of change – offer to call back, if lengthy directions to find you are required

- springs on you a question you haven't had before: 'Are you clean?', 'Is there a view?', 'Tell me about your hotel', 'Are there log fires?'

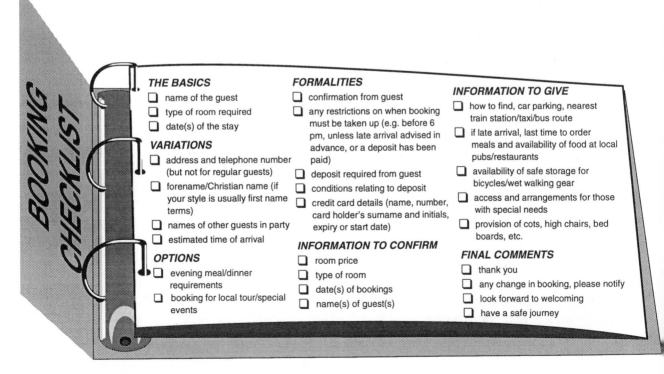

BOOKING CHECKLIST

THE BASICS
- ☐ name of the guest
- ☐ type of room required
- ☐ date(s) of the stay

VARIATIONS
- ☐ address and telephone number (but not for regular guests)
- ☐ forename/Christian name (if your style is usually first name terms)
- ☐ names of other guests in party
- ☐ estimated time of arrival

OPTIONS
- ☐ evening meal/dinner requirements
- ☐ booking for local tour/special events

FORMALITIES
- ☐ confirmation from guest
- ☐ any restrictions on when booking must be taken up (e.g. before 6 pm, unless late arrival advised in advance, or a deposit has been paid)
- ☐ deposit required from guest
- ☐ conditions relating to deposit
- ☐ credit card details (name, number, card holder's surname and initials, expiry or start date)

INFORMATION TO CONFIRM
- ☐ room price
- ☐ type of room
- ☐ date(s) of bookings
- ☐ name(s) of guest(s)

INFORMATION TO GIVE
- ☐ how to find, car parking, nearest train station/taxi/bus route
- ☐ if late arrival, last time to order meals and availability of food at local pubs/restaurants
- ☐ availability of safe storage for bicycles/wet walking gear
- ☐ access and arrangements for those with special needs
- ☐ provision of cots, high chairs, bed boards, etc.

FINAL COMMENTS
- ☐ thank you
- ☐ any change in booking, please notify
- ☐ look forward to welcoming
- ☐ have a safe journey

Establish your approach

A booking is a contract:

- you agree to provide a service – accommodation, breakfast, etc.

- and the guest agrees to pay for it.

Even when not confirmed in writing, a legal contract exists. But the problem is proving it, should the guest default. Another is the effort required to win compensation.

One route is to go for maximum protection: all bookings confirmed in writing by both you and the guest, and a deposit taken, non-refundable in the event of a no-show or late cancellation. Or you decide on a flexible approach:

1 regulars: telephone confirmation sufficient, address/telephone number not requested (already on file)

2 new guests: address, telephone number and estimated time of arrival requested, brochure sent with informal note confirming booking

3 at busy times, new guests asked to confirm the booking with a deposit.

An approach favoured by hotel groups, is to obtain credit card details in return for a 'guaranteed reservation'. In the event of a no-show, the guest is charged for the first night (at least).

When colleagues or staff take bookings, do explain what exceptions can be allowed. Such as not asking a cyclist calling from a nearby public telephone box for an address and telephone number (no, you explain, not the call box number but a home number).

Expensive mistake

Having taken a booking for a single room on a night when the hotel was already full, by mistake, Darryl Gregory, proprietor of the Hotel On the Park, Cheltenham, tried to contact the guest. All attempts failed. There was little chance of another cancellation, so Gregory booked the guest into a nearby 4-star hotel. When the guest arrived, the mistake was apologised for, the arrangements explained (which included paying the extra £40 it would cost to stay at the other hotel), complimentary drinks offered, and an offer to "make up for our unfortunate mistake by way of dinner or something similar" on the second night, when a room at the Hotel On the Park was available. The guest decided to stay at the other hotel, and Gregory again paid the £40 difference.

On checking out, the guest had his bill for more than £200 sent to the Hotel On the Park. Gregory had no choice but to settle this (on top of the £80 he had already paid). Reluctantly he sent the guest a bill for the equivalent of two nights in a single room at the Hotel On the Park.

The response was a letter from the guest stating that he was seeking damages. "We were shocked and amazed. What damages?" asked Gregory. "The hotel that he was booked out to was 10 minutes down the road. He had not wanted dinner at either hotel, had chosen the cheapest room, at a special discount offer, and was clearly not looking for a hotel experience."

Gregory had to take the case to county court, where he was awarded the outstanding bill, but the judge also awarded £100 damages to the guest and ordered each side to pay their own costs.

Darryl Gregory writing in Viewpoint, *Caterer & Hotelkeeper*

Taking a deposit

Consider what size deposit you should ask for, your policy on what will happen to the deposit when a guest cancels or fails to turn up, and how to communicate these 'terms and conditions' in a business-like, but friendly way. Some questions to help the process:

- what size deposit should you ask for? Below £5 is more trouble than it is worth, too high a sum and it is beginning to look like payment in advance

- if the guest cancels giving you a reasonable time to relet the room, do you return all or some of the deposit? It would usually be acceptable to keep a deposit of £10 or less, because of the time spent handling the booking, postal expenses and bank charges. For larger sums, it would also be acceptable to retain a portion for the same reasons. Keeping large deposits may require justification in court, if the aggrieved guest pursues matters.

For the no-show, the retained deposit protects your loss of profits. It may be considered unreasonable to keep all of a large deposit, as you have not had the expense of breakfast, cleaning the room, and laundering the bed linen.

The guest-friendly options include:

- inviting the guest to re-book on another date, in which case the deposit is transferred

- returning most or all the deposit to those who cancel in reasonable time, or for genuine circumstances (e.g. illness), in the hope that these guests will stay on a future occasion.

Allocate rooms to maximise revenue

How well does your system for matching guest requirements to rooms available work? With greater flexibility, can you increase room revenue overall?

For example, do you move Mr Robert's booking (a regular) for a standard single for a week to a twin with private bath at no extra charge, so that you can accept a cyclist's booking for a standard single for one night?

arguments for

— demand for singles is always strong at that time of the year, so you should be able to sell the standard single on the other nights

— it is better to upgrade a regular guest than let the twin at a discount to chance guests for single occupancy

— it takes less time and costs less to clean a standard single room after a departure than a twin room

— you have other twins and doubles available to meet extra demand

risks

— you will have to refuse bookings for the twin at the full price

— no one else will require the standard single

— the regular guests likes the single because it is at the back of the hotel, whereas the twin is at the front, and there is some street noise

— the regular might expect to be upgraded on future visits when the twin room has not been let.

When a guest must have a specific room, note this clearly in your reservations book so that you or someone else does not move that person to accommodate another booking.

Get a feel for what guests want

Having stated the prices of your rooms, there is a long silence ... are you too cheap or too expensive? People used to city hotel prices, or business accounts, may link lower prices to poor quality. Better value and better service is the case you need to make. Provide reassurance: describe the facilities, send a brochure.

Guests on a tight budget, may be persuaded by good value, e.g. your price includes a substantial breakfast. Or you may be able to offer a budget room, or a lower price because business is quiet.

Help guests you cannot accommodate

When you are full, or your prices are higher than the person wants to pay, or there are other reasons you cannot take a booking, end the conversation on a friendly note, e.g. 'I'm very sorry we are not able to help on this occasion'. Ask if the caller has other places to try, or can you give some numbers?

If everywhere is likely to be booked, get this information into the conversation – with tact. You want the caller to try you on a future visit because you are helpful. Avoid taunts: 'You'll be lucky to find anywhere. Around here is always booked up months in advance.' An option is to say 'Unfortunately, it's very difficult to find accommodation while the motor show at Newark is on. The Tourist Information Centre there keeps track of any availability, the number is .... Alternatively, you will find it easier further north or south.'

Two other things you don't want to do:

- lose a regular guest: explain why you are full, offer an upgrade if available

- the person to feel that you have given poor advice, e.g. because the suggested place is very noisy: give options and factual not judgemental comments, e.g. 'and there's the Bell, a pub on the high street, or Mrs Wilson, a B&B, on the outskirts of the town...'

Develop a good relationship with other accommodation providers, so that you can direct your overflow in their direction, and they do the reverse. Pick places not in direct competition, with clear differences to what you provide, e.g. no bar, restricted meals. Then when you have to send regulars elsewhere, they will appreciate all the more what you offer.

4 Negotiate to win business

Bargaining for hotel rooms is catching on. More guests are looking for the best offer, just as you do when buying catering equipment or a holiday abroad. Those booking for a group are particularly alert to the opportunities for negotiating a discount.

A bill which is higher than the guest expects can undo all the good impressions you have created during the stay. To avoid this, be clear from the start what the price includes, and any special conditions.

Be aware of guest expectations on price: if breakfast is extra, or the price only includes a continental breakfast, state this on your tariff, and when taking a booking.

Avoid the 'from £X' price, which few guests can take advantage of (e.g. because you only have one small single at this rate), or which is misleading (e.g. because most rooms have private bathrooms and are much more expensive).

The case for negotiating

There is a case for negotiating – unless you are certain to fill all your rooms at the full price, and unless the guest in question is unlikely to be put off future visits by your inflexibility. Certainly, you cannot turn the clock back: rooms unsold on any night are not able to be stored like a bottle of wine to sell on a future occasion. The revenue is lost forever. Some other points to consider:

- what the guest pays above the costs of cleaning the room, laundry and providing breakfast is gross profit

- what the guest might spend in the bar, on wine and food is also profit

- what the likelihood is of other guests requiring accommodation for the period, and how much will they pay?

- for bookings via travel agents, tourist information centres and other third parties: whether you want this business and can you afford the discount/commission (not less than 10%)

- what the effect will be on your image: will discounted prices attract the wrong guests?

- what the long term effect will be: once you start offering discounts, you increase the expectation that all prices are negotiable.

Establish a framework

Make a record of agreed discounts, and the conditions to which they apply. Otherwise, matters get out of control:

- returning guests query why they are paying more than on a previous visit

- you find you have given larger discounts than you need.

Value for children

At the Coppid Beech Hotel, children are asked to fill in separate check-in forms at a low-level check-in desk. They become automatic members of the Bobby Beech Nut Club, and receive a pack of colouring pens and books. Dates of birth are noted to send birthday cards.

Peter Kalinke, proprietor of the 10-room Dove Hotel in Brighton often goes into the kitchen to make a snack for families who arrive with children hungry after a long journey.

Some approaches to charging for children

- children under specified age (e.g. 12) sharing adult room free, nominal charge for breakfast

- sliding scale, e.g. under 3 years old 10% of adult rate, under 7 years old 20%, 7 to 14 years old, 50%.

Caterer & Hotelkeeper

Do not confuse guests

Decide what discounts, if any, you should tell guests about in your brochure, advertisements, etc. Keep it simple, clear, and concentrate on the offers that will attract extra business. Remember, anyone asking for a discount is likely to expect something better than any advertised rate.

Take as an example, the offer of a fifth night free, a feature of many city breaks. The majority of people on city breaks want a two- or three-day stay, but there are some who can be tempted to stay longer by such an offer. The terms are quite clear. On the other hand, offering a discount of 20% off the accommodation charges for stays of five nights or longer, although equivalent in value, opens the door to further negotiations. 'I only want to stay four nights, so can I have 15% discount?'

ARE PRICES ADVERTISED

- ☐ in reception (by law, potential guests should be able to find out the room charge from a price list displayed in reception or at the entrance of the building)?
- ☐ in guest room information?

ARE PRICES CLEAR

- ☐ what is included, e.g. service, VAT, breakfast?
- ☐ what is excluded, e.g. room only?
- ☐ extras, e.g. child sharing parents' room, meals served in the room?
- ☐ surcharges, e.g. single occupancy of double/twin, sea view?
- ☐ for hotel services, e.g. telephone calls, viewing film chanel on TV, meals for children, use of leisure facilities?
- ☐ reflect guest expectations: no unpleasant shocks on the bill?

WILL DISCOUNTS

- ☐ attract new business: longer stays, new guests, groups, business at off-peak periods?
- ☐ give you adequate profit margin?
- ☐ attract the kind of guests you want?
- ☐ not adversely impact on existing business?

ARE PAYMENT TERMS CLEAR

- ☐ including which credit cards you accept, and if there is a surcharge?
- ☐ that cheques require a bank guarantee card, or prior arrangement?
- ☐ credit terms available to account customers?
- ☐ when payment is expected from travel agents/other third parties?

Do you, or do you not, take dogs?

The Lake Country House Hotel, near Builth Wells in Powys attracts many animal lovers. Owners Jean-Pierre and Jan Mifsud believe firmly that allowing dogs at the hotel boosts their revenue. "Dog people do not to go abroad so much. If they can take a break with their dog, then they tend to come to the likes of us."

At the Thornbury Castle Hotel, dogs are not welcome. "I love dogs" explains proprietor Maurice Taylor. "But I don't see why people going to a hotel room should have to sleep where a dog has slept." Taylor further rules out dogs staying overnight in their owner's cars or hotel kennels, "Unhappy dogs cry and bark all night – our customers come here for tranquillity."

Sara Guild reporting in *Caterer & Hotelkeeper*

Doorstep negotiating

Someone has called at the door without a booking. You give the price for a single, the person asks to see the room. The reaction is rather non-committal. What you next suspect, happens. 'Can you give me a better price?'

Or having agreed you believe, to take the room, the person asks for a reduction because no breakfast will be required.

Think through the options in advance, to prepare for such situations:

- how much do you want the guest(s) to stay, judging on what you see: behaviour, attitude and appearance?

- what is the likelihood of other guests requiring the room?

- is providing breakfast an essential part of the experience of guests staying at your place?

- having offered a reduction, will more be demanded?

- is this someone with a clearly unrealistic expectation of the cost of accommodation?

- is the person likely to spend generously on food and drinks?

- is this a compulsive negotiator, who will tour the area if necessary?

- what happens if the children, said not to eat any breakfast, have eggs, bacon, sausage, mushrooms, tomato, fried bread and demolish piles of toast?

Reduced rates for long-term stay

The Novar Arms in Ross-shire boosted its occupancy from 28.6% in February to almost 70% in March, thanks to 13 steel fixers staying at the hotel until September. The men are paying just £10 a night per person for a bed and £7 a day per person for breakfast and a set early evening meal.

Proprietor Robin Murray agrees that the rate sounds bad, and admits he was sorely tempted to turn down the business. But the men are sharing the unrefurbished twin rooms and are drinking copious amounts at the bar. Suddenly £34 per room, seven days a week for six months sounds attractive – and that's not to mention the bar bills.

Angela Jameson reporting in *Caterer & Hotelkeeper*

5 Respond to special requests

When asked for something out of the ordinary, do you say 'no' – but what impression does this give? Do you say 'yes' – but wonder what are you letting yourself in for? Or do you give the request a few moments thought, and reply as helpfully as possible?

When a guest has a special need, or makes an unusual request, this is your opportunity to excel.

Some guests expect, and some demand, to be treated specially. They may not even say 'thank you'. But the majority really do appreciate your help, will say so, tell others, and become regular guests.

Be positive in your approach. Even when the solution is not immediately apparent, and the problems seem overwhelming, creative thinking can produce a solution. Discussion with the guest and with colleagues often helps point the way forward.

Recognise a special need

'Special needs' is a useful umbrella term to cover all those with mobility and/or communication difficulties. It avoids the negative associations of words like 'handicapped'. It can be usefully extended to include the elderly, children, women on their own, and anyone else who has or might have different needs from the majority of your other guests.

This is the crux: providing for the individual or the minority. If most of your guests are families with children, then an adult who feels uncomfortable surrounded by children has a special need. In a hotel with mostly elderly people, those younger by a few decades or more have a special need.

- Borrow a wheelchair.
- Sit in it and propel yourself around the guest areas of the building.
- Include the toilets, bedrooms, restaurant and bar, in and out of the main entrance and so forth.
- Make a note of restrictions and difficulties as you experience them.
- Then use your list to make an action plan to overcome as many as practicable.

Taking the special need viewpoint

Avoid assumptions, ask questions, listen, observe and where possible, try to experience. The attitude you and your staff show to guests with special needs is what really counts. A willingness to understand and do your best to provide for those needs is what really matters.

When you have to say 'no'

Do not offer what you cannot provide. Tell parents if your place is not ideal for young children, perhaps because the unprotected fish pond means they must be constantly supervised. Be clear about the annex which is a short walk from the main building, the no parking restriction, and anything else of this sort.

> ### Access for all
>
> Over 30,000 requests are made each year to the charity, Holiday Care, to match people with disabilities to premises able to cope with their physical demands. To accommodate such people need not mean expensive alterations. It can be done by colour schemes to aid those with partial sight, or providing talking menus for people with impaired hearing and building ramps into public areas. Information on the Accessible Standards, and other advice is available from the tourist boards.

Caterer & Hotelkeeper

Helping those with a special need: some do's

- Be sensitive to, and on the alert for, those who have a special need.
- Offer to help, guide and explain. But recognise the need to be independent and be patient.
- Attract the person's attention before you speak, e.g. call by name, gently tap on shoulder.
- Talk naturally. When not understood, say it another way. Tactfully check that you have been understood.
- When a guest has difficulty managing food, offer to bone fish or meat dishes, and cut up lettuce, baked potatoes, etc.

Some don'ts

- Don't talk down, patronise, or address all your remarks to a companion unless this is obviously preferred.
- Don't make decisions on behalf of special needs guests without consulting them or their carer.
- Don't pet or play with guide dogs.
- Don't overfill cups or glasses. Warn about very hot liquids, or dishes.
- Don't put special needs guests at undesirable tables, in un-popular or sub-standard rooms.
- When asked to repeat what you have said, do not say 'it doesn't matter', or 'it's not important': this leads to frustration.
- Avoid inappropriate or exaggerated facial expressions, but relevant gestures can help.

Wheelchair users

- Is there space for the wheel-chair user to move along corridors, use the facilities in toilets and bathrooms, get into and out of bed from the wheelchair, sit in comfort for meals, in the lounge, etc.?
- Can the registration book, menu, etc. be easily reached sitting in a wheelchair?

Visually impaired

- When you meet the guest, say who you are. When you walk away, say that you are going.
- Offer to help: don't assume the person needs a guiding hand. Don't be afraid to ask 'how much can you see?'
- To guide a blind guest, offer your arm. Say when you get to a kerb or steps and whether to go up or down. Mention hazards and whether they are to the left or right. Place the person's hand on the back of the chair (to get orientated before sitting).
- Be careful not to leave doors ajar and put things back where you found them.
- Describe the surroundings: knowing why particular sounds or smells are coming from different parts of the room will help the guest relax.
- Provide helpful facilities, e.g. light switches in bright colours, door numbers which can be read by touch, telephone for the visually impaired, emergency notices and information pack in braille.
- Touch before you speak, serve a drink or food. Touch is the way that blind people see. Say what the food is when you serve it and describe its position on the plate using the hands of a clock, e.g. meat at three o'clock.
- Tell the guest what the bill total is, and ask if you can itemise the different charges. Identify change as you hand it back to the guest.

Deaf or hard of hearing

- Keep your rhythm of speech normal but a little slower. Speak clearly and in plain language. Do not shout: this distorts the lip pattern and can cause pain to hearing aid users; shouting can also be embarrassing and makes any conversation strained.
- Look directly at the guest when talking, and do not obscure your mouth, e.g. by waving a pen or hand in front of it. Keep head and body movements to the minimum.
- Make sure that light is on your face. Avoid standing with your back to a window or bright light (which makes it difficult for the person to see your face).
- Start your sentence with a word or two which will give the lip-reader the context of what you are about to say.

Speech difficulty

- Avoid correcting the guest or trying to take over the conversation.
- Ask short questions that can be quickly answered or only require a nod or other gesture.
- Do not pretend to understand something that you don't. If necessary, repeat what you understand, checking from the guest's reaction whether or not you are right.

Young children

- Offer a cot in the bedroom, a high chair or cushion to sit on in the restaurant.
- In the restaurant, sit the child where he or she can see what is going on. Offer smaller portions. Provide extra napkins, small glasses (of the plain, tumbler type).
- Put a family with children in a room and at a restaurant table where any noise will least disturb other customers.
- Serve children their drink, bread roll, snack, etc. as quickly as possible – children soon become impatient.

A woman on her own

- Consider which room provides most comfort and security, i.e. not down a corridor past many other rooms, or in an annex.

Special diets

- Don't claim that a dish is suitable for certain diets, but tell the guest all the ingredients and cooking method.
- Aim for variety in dishes and a wide range of ingredients and cooking methods: those on a special diet can then choose what they will enjoy.

With thanks to The Royal National Institute for Deaf People and the Royal National Institute for the Blind

Pet owners

Your experience of a guest's dog or cat, can be disastrously at odds with the owner's assurance that it is 'small, very well behaved'. Establish some ground rules:

- which pets you will not accept: snakes, parrots, spiders, tarantulas, etc.

- what if any extra charge will be made

- that the animal must be in the control of the owners when it is in public places

- that other guests should not be disturbed: by barking, howling or other unwelcome noises

- that you will expect guests to pay for any damage their pets make.

When you do not accept pets, state this (discreetly) in your brochure, or other information sent to guests before their arrival. For enquiries, have details available of other hotels in the area which are pet-friendly or suggest pet owners contact the tourist information centre.

The number of people following special diets is rising, writes Mabel Blades in *Food Service Management*. The strictures of religious teaching, medical needs and personal ethics means that, knowingly or otherwise, most food service operations will be feeding someone with special needs.

If in doubt, check what people can or cannot eat.

Ethical diets

Vegetarian – excludes any type of meat or fish, milk products and eggs are usually acceptable, some may eat fish (where the main concern is the farming and slaughter of animals)

Vegan – more rigid form of vegetarianism in that its adherents avoid all food derived from animals or fish, including dairy produce and eggs: use soya milk and vegetable spreads

Religious diets

Muslim – all pork, shellfish and alcohol products are forbidden. Meat must be Halal (slaughtered according to custom)

Hindu – orthodox Hindus are usually strict vegetarians and eat no meat, fish or eggs. Less strict Hindus may eat lamb, poultry and fish but definitely not beef, as cattle have a deep religious meaning. Milk, however, is highly regarded

Sikh – Lamb, poultry and fish are usually acceptable to the men, whilst a strong vegetarian tradition exists among Sikh women

Jewish – avoid pork products, shellfish and eels. Strict Jews will eat only Kosher meat which is slaughtered according to tradition. Meat and milk must not be served at the same meal or cooked together

Rastafarian – based on an Ital diet, food only in its natural state is consumed so any processed food is forbidden. They do not eat pork, fish without fins (eels) alcohol, coffee or tea

Medical diets

Diabetes – low sugar, low fat, high fibre and for insulin injected diabetics, plenty of starchy carbohydrates: potatoes, pasta, rice or cous-cous

Low cholesterol and **saturated fat** – there are only a few high-cholesterol foods, notably liver, egg yolks and shellfish. Beef, pork and lamb do not contain much cholesterol, but do contain saturated fats. Saturated fats to avoid are butter, cream, margarine and red meat

Low fat – people with gall bladder or liver disorders find eating any kind of fat can cause pain

Coeliac – avoids gluten, a protein commonly found in wheat, thus avoid anything made with wheat flour, including pasta, bread and pastries. There is no problem with rice, potato, corn and sago

Nut allergy – nut oils are often blended into other oils and margarines, so it is better to use pure oils and butter

With thanks to *Food Service Management*

6 Welcome arrivals

The quality of welcome sets the mood for the guest's stay with you. Without doubt it is an important moment. Done well, it creates a fund of goodwill. Done poorly, it may overshadow everything else that follows.

A smile creates a friendly, welcoming impression. Eye contact implies interest. A deliberate upright posture implies confidence and enthusiasm.

From what you know of arriving guests – likely time of arrival, number in party, where they have come from, etc. – you should be able to greet most guests by name.

A genuinely helpful attitude, when nothing is too much trouble, distinguishes the excellent guesthouse, farmhouse, inn or B&B. Tourist board, AA and RAC inspectors also look for well-trained, knowledgeable and enthusiastic proprietors and staff, showing very good levels of attention and anticipating guests' needs.

The first impression

To give a good welcome requires a range of skills, so that you can deal with the guests who are nervous, shy, timid, unfriendly, bad tempered or downright hostile. You must also overcome your own feelings – a challenge when the guest's arrival coincides with a crisis in the kitchen or a visit by the fire officer.

Consider what contributes to the first impression a guest will get and what can go wrong. Then develop simple rules for yourself and anyone else who greets guests on arrival. Some questions to get the process going:

- is it clear where newly arrived guests should go (i.e. if there is more than one door into the building)?

- if the front door is locked, will the door bell be heard and answered quickly (even if you are cleaning or checking one of the guest bedrooms)?

- is it clear how guests can get your attention (if reception is not staffed all the time)?

- do you prepare a list of the names of arriving guests, how many in the party, expected time of arrival, and the rooms they will be in?

- are staff told the names of arriving guests and is every new arrival greeted in a friendly, polite way?

- are those who are not guests, not looking for accommodation, not known to you, asked for identification (e.g. sales representatives, survey researchers)?

That all-round impression

Creating a positive impression when the guest first enters the hotel and registers is widely acknowledged as vital. But this can be quickly undone by 'moments of truth' – seemingly obscure incidents, overlooked by management, such as finding the route to the bedroom littered with used linen.

Positive 'moments of truth' can also occur, when management and staff are genuinely focused on quality service. Examples include:

- on arrival, being offered an upgrade from a single to a double room

- on departure, being asked whether a taxi is required

- arriving on a wet and wintry night, entering your bedroom to find it warm, the curtains already drawn and side lamp switched on.

Bob Lillis writing in *Caterer & Hotelkeeper*

Please your guests

Arrivals without a booking

Experience has to be your guide. If you are in an area popular with overseas tourists, and touring British holidaymakers, chance arrivals may be one of your main sources of business.

Unfortunately, some proprietors have less happy experiences with chance arrivals. Failure to pay the bill, use of a stolen credit card or cheque book, theft of your or other guests' property, disruptive behaviour, damage to property and people, have become familiar problems.

One tactic in this situation is to avoid indicating that you have accommodation available, until you are satisfied that you wish the person to stay. Following a question along the lines of 'Have you a room available?', you can buy time by asking what sort of room the person is looking for, and for how many nights.

If you are immediately doubtful, it is easier to say no if you keep the person on the doorstep (but preferably not in the rain!). Another tactic is to quote the most expensive room.

Of course, you are taking part in a two-way situation. The price or the room(s) or some other feature may not be acceptable to the caller.

Questions you might ask yourself before accepting a chance guest:

* what can you judge from appearance, attitude, eye contact, method of arrival?

* is the reason for the visit plausible: is the project a 'contractor' speaks of really going on, is it likely that someone would be researching local history?

* what luggage does the person have? Walkers and cyclists would usually have belongings with them.

Saying no because you have no rooms available

A helpful approach creates goodwill for your town, city or locality, and for you. On a future visit you want the person to stay with you: offer a brochure or card, so that an advance booking can be made.

Goodwill can also be created among your fellow businesses, by telephoning them to see if they have suitable accommodation available. Be cautious that this does not backfire, when the guest behaves in some 'unacceptable' way to a less tolerant proprietor.

Saying no because you want to

Soften the impact of your 'no' by suggesting other places where accommodation can be found. Stick to general advice, e.g. 'there are several places in the high street', or 'the newsagent's window has a number of advertisements of nearby B&Bs'. Nevertheless, the person may claim at the next place that you have recommended it. Your fellow proprietor should see through this line.

When you are convinced someone is a swindler, seek the advice of the police, as other hotels and guesthouses may have reported incidents. Use any formal or informal network for exchanging such information with fellow businesses.

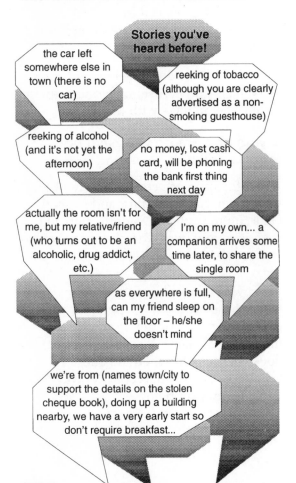

Stories you've heard before!

- the car left somewhere else in town (there is no car)
- reeking of tobacco (although you are clearly advertised as a non-smoking guesthouse)
- reeking of alcohol (and it's not yet the afternoon)
- no money, lost cash card, will be phoning the bank first thing next day
- actually the room isn't for me, but my relative/friend (who turns out to be an alcoholic, drug addict, etc.)
- I'm on my own... a companion arrives some time later, to share the single room
- as everywhere is full, can my friend sleep on the floor – he/she doesn't mind
- we're from (names town/city to support the details on the stolen cheque book), doing up a building nearby, we have a very early start so don't require breakfast...

Hedging your bets

Having decided, on balance, to accept a chance guest, you can reduce the risk of a misjudgement by:

- confirming limited availability, e.g. 'yes I do have a single for tonight', and if a longer stay is requested, 'well I can help with a single for tonight, but at the moment that room is booked for the rest of the week' (later, if your fears prove groundless, you can say there has been a cancellation, and the room is now free)

- asking for payment in advance: some guests offer this (because they are used to staying in places which demand it)

- checking credit cards, cheque guarantee cards and cheques carefully: phoning the credit card company/bank in case of doubt

- checking that the car registration number matches the one the guest gave when signing in, and making a note of the make and colour of car.

'Guests' check in to burgle other guests

Two or three men, smartly dressed, aged between 35 and 50, using French names and addresses, have been checking into London hotels, paying cash in advance for a night's stay, then going on a thieving spree around other guests' rooms. Cameras, jewellery and a fur coat were among the items stolen.

Police advised hoteliers to change locks regularly, thoroughly check passport numbers and be aware of unexpected guests.

Caterer & Hotelkeeper

Please your guests

Keep a look out for signs that will confirm or allay your suspicions:

- incomplete or implausible address or car registration number

- no car registration number, no sign of car

- asking to cash a cheque

- extravagance, ordering the best wines, etc.

- none or very little luggage/personal possessions in the room

- nervous, edgy behaviour.

Take-ins and take-aways

A guest, faced with a cold pizza and nowhere obvious to heat it, found a new use for the trouser press. The next morning, it took the housekeeper some time to work out why there was a gooey mess under the trouser press.

Staff at the Rowardennan Hotel at Loch Lomond, had a bit of a shock when this very thin, bedraggled man staggered into the restaurant and promptly ordered soup, lasagne and chips. He said this was the first meal he had eaten after a month-long fast, camping in the hills. Much concerned by his appearance, the hotel staff rang for an ambulance to take the man to hospital, but when it arrived he insisted on first finishing his meal.

Table Talk, *Caterer & Hotelkeeper*

The practicalities

On the guest's arrival, certain formalities and courtesies have to be dealt with:

1 Ask the guest to register

- by law the minimum requirement is for full name and nationality and date of arrival for every guest aged 16 years or over (even those sharing a room)

- for non-British guests, a record must also be kept of the number of their passport or equivalent identity document. Before or on departure, non-British guests must tell you their next destination and if known, the full address there

- registration details can be given by any member of the party on behalf of the others, or a third party such as the tour guide

- if your style is to call most guests by their forename, this is a good time to find what it is, perhaps by a remark in a friendly tone 'what does the "T" stand for?'

- for regulars, you can simplify registration by completing the form or entry for them, asking them to check the details and sign

- for security, and for your mailing list, ask guests if you may add the postcode or other details they have omitted; if this irritates them, give a reason such as 'only yesterday we had difficulty returning lost property because of an incomplete address'

- also for security, obtain the car registration number

- for practical reasons, obtain the date of departure; query any difference from the information given at the time of booking.

2 Check method of payment (optional)

- this focuses guests on how they intend paying, and any problems can be sorted in advance of the departure, e.g. payment by cheque when the bill total is certain to be over the cheque guarantee limit

- an additional safeguard is to complete a credit card voucher, and ask the guest to sign it, ready for the final total to be entered at the end of the stay

- a guest who has booked through a travel agent, tourist information centre or other third party, can be asked to produce the voucher – having this at the beginning rather than the end of the stay, makes it easier to get the bill correct.

3 Offer assistance with luggage

- an opportunity to demonstrate the personal touch, and to get to know the guests better.

4 Show the guest to the room

- usually combined with 3, and for the guest who has little luggage or wants to bring it from the car later, it is another opportunity to give personal service – few hotels below 5-star rating from the large companies bother to do this

- on your way to the room, and once there, you can point out facilities, ask what time breakfast will be required, explain how to control the heating, the TV and alarm clock, and security information (e.g. their own key to the front door, storage of valuables)

- often by chatting to guests, you can find out why they chose your place to stay, what they have come to the area for, and pick up clues on the information which would help them enjoy their stay more (see page 5).

The quality welcome

Much of 3 and 4 is about providing a quality welcome. If you do not do so already, consider offering (complimentary) tea or coffee on arrival. You provide another opportunity to get to know the guests, and make them feel welcome. The effort and cost is small, and equivalent to or less than the guest using the in-room facilities to make his/her own.

Telephone calls and messages for guests

Mail or messages can be handed over at registration (unless you have left them in the room, in which case it is courteous to tell the guest this on arrival). By using a duplicate pad for messages, you can put one copy in the guest's room, and keep the second copy to give to guests when you next see them.

Anyone answering the phone should have a list of guest names. Ask the caller to hold while you check if the guest is available. If not, offer to take a message.

Get the name of the guest's caller, so that you can tell the guest who is on the phone. This helps the guest prepare mentally. Otherwise the time between knowing there is a call, and speaking to the caller can cause alarm: is there a problem at home? at work?

Award-winning landlady

Muriel Orme, AA Landlady of the Year award-winner, takes a personal interest in her guests' welfare. Rooms at her B&B in Oakamoor, Staffordshire, are hotel-like in their comfort and spaciousness. But few hotels would or could offer the assistance that she gives.

She will pick guests up at the station 18 miles away, drop them off and collect them from the local pub, and take them back to the station via the scenic route, acting as guide and friend. She cooks dinner when requested and likes to discuss the menu in advance.

Worried about the itinerary of an American couple, she was, typically, observed making several telephone calls on their behalf and sending them on their way with a much-improved route. It left an indelible impression of British hospitality at its best.

Joe Hyam, reporting in *Caterer & Hotelkeeper*

---

7 Deal with problem guests

Guests who complain, are a bit difficult or irritate you in some way or another cause a mild disturbance in the daily pattern of life. Hopefully, the real problem guests are far fewer in number, but the devastating effect they have can take a long time to recover from. To recognise the problem early on can help. So will the basic rules on how to handle conflict, violence, drunkenness and other difficult situations.

Experience of people is your best guide. Look out for anything unusual, which does not match what you know of the guest. Appearance, behaviour, questions asked, things said – these can all be clues.

When you have had some problem with a guest, reflect back on how you handled it. With the benefit of hindsight, it is much easier to identify the warning signs. You become 'older and wiser', better prepared to avoid a similar situation in the future.

Spot the warning signs

On its own, the unusual address, the question about how late guests can come in, the friend who wasn't staying, the clinking of bottles from the off-licence may have meant nothing. When the guest has gone without paying, taken the room and front door keys, the room has obviously been used by two people, and red wine has been spilt over the bed and carpet, you want to kick yourself for not spotting trouble.

A warning sign is not conclusive. You may even be wrong. Nevertheless, you can go on extra alert. Perhaps watching the guest more closely, taking extra care with the master keys and money, waiting up until everyone has gone to their room.

Get into conversation with the guest. Take the opportunity to ask apparently innocent questions to find out more about the guest. Reluctance to talk may indicate nothing more than shyness or a determination to protect privacy. Extreme talkativeness may be a cover.

Certain types of guest have more potential for trouble. Groups of people (same sex or mixed sex) determined to enjoy themselves often take their lead from the worst behaved among them.

> **No money, no award**
>
> After failing to pay a £360 bill for two nights over New Year at the Kensington Park Hotel, a 32-year-old man was conditionally discharged for a year. Magistrates heard that the man has spent most of the time since the offences undergoing mental treatment. No money was awarded to the hotel, since his means were insufficient to pay.

Caterer & Hotelkeeper

Limit the problem

One solution is not to accept guests who might cause a problem: no groups, no football supporters, no stag night guests, no motorcyclists, no students, no workmen or contractors, no one wearing trainers/jeans/leathers. But you lose the business, and you miss out on the decent people to be found in any of these categories.

Another solution is to lay down lots of rules: front door locked at 11.30 pm, no visitors in rooms after 10 pm, no take-away food or carry-outs from the off-licence to be consumed on the premises. But this can be counter-productive, and guests attempt to climb up drain pipes, or smuggle in 'forbidden' items.

The third route is to be alert to, and react quickly to, each individual situation. You can:

- find out more about a group before accepting the booking, talk to the motorcyclists, get to know the students' tutors

- politely ask rowdy guests to be quieter as they are disturbing other guests (or the neighbours)

- speak to the leader of the party about any troublemakers or bad behaviour

- offer a table, plates, knives and forks and suggest take-aways are eaten in the dining room – the bedroom and corridors won't smell of food, no risk of spills on the bed linen, you can dispose promptly of the remnants

- ask heavy-spending or long stay guests to pay an interim bill

- phone the credit card company or bank for authorisation of a payment, to check that the card or cheque book was not stolen, to arrange express clearance of a cheque

- check guest rooms – if they are in, make an excuse, e.g. that the central heating has been misbehaving, and you are checking all radiators.

Keep to a low-key, calm, polite but firm approach. Avoid getting into an argument with guests. Don't match anger with anger.

Don't risk your safety

Should the problem get out of control, call the police. Do not take the law into your own hands. Concentrate on getting descriptions of the people involved and any other information which will help the police.

Police estimate that an average hotel loses 12% of its towels through theft every year. Some house-keepers say it could be more than double that.

Angry owner ignores gunman danger

Going against the advice of the police in such a situation, Magbool Chaudry, owner of the Khyber Pass in Aberdeen refused to hand over cash when a man wearing a balaclava came into the restaurant and pointed a handgun at his head. 'I was numb for about 20 seconds and then I ran into the kitchen for help', he said. 'I was really angry. You work so hard for your living and he wasn't going to take it away.'

Fortunately for Chaudry and the two kitchen assistants who came to his help, the gunman, described as being about 25, chubby or fat and with dark hair, fled.

Caterer & Hotelkeeper

Your legal obligations

You are responsible for the health and safety of everyone on the premises. You must not knowingly put anyone at risk. Difficult problems have arisen for hoteliers when drunk guests have fallen out of windows or tampered with fire detectors. Someone who is drunk and smokes is a fire risk.

If you sell alcohol, then as licensee you have a responsibility not to sell alcohol to anyone under age, or to permit drunkenness in the bar.

It is an offence to discriminate on the grounds of sex, race or disability.

Serious accidents and injury involving staff, and in certain situations guests, should be reported to your environmental health department. Some diseases are reportable.

A♣ Deal with agression or violence

1♣ recognise the warning signs: unusual behaviour, higher-pitched voice, aggressive gestures, rowdy or silly behaviour, sudden silences

2♣ counteract frustration: don't ignore anyone waiting, apologise for delays or problems, avoid unguarded remarks or misdirected humorous comment

3♣ take the heat out of the situation: talk calmly, slowly and deliberately in your normal tone of voice (control vocal signals of anxiety and stress), allow the person to talk and express anger, avoid or respond indirectly to angry or hostile remarks, express understanding of the aggressor's situation

4♣ control your body language: appear relaxed, avoid prolonged eye contact or aggressive gestures, maintain a careful distance, make any movement slow and deliberate

5♣ if possible, move the person away from other guests

6♣ make it clear what you want to happen: for the person to behave, stop drinking, to leave

7♣ depersonalise the encounter: emphasise your obligations to the law and to other guests, or use excuses which can't be challenged, e.g. the banks have asked us to take more care

8♣ give the person the opportunity to back down without losing face

9♣ do not hesitate to call the police if you need help

News story

A conman, described as 42 years old, of slim build with gaunt features, receding brown hair, well educated, and with an interest in architecture, ran up bills of almost £400 for a single night at 4-star hotels in Powys and Gloucestershire.

When Llangoed Hall checked the credit card, they were told there was a problem and refused to accept payment. The man left his passport as security and went into the town to collect cash. He failed to return. The passport had also been obtained falsely.

Caterer & Hotelkeeper

Please your guests

Protect your reputation

Locally and among your other guests, your reputation will be harmed by disorderly behaviour, noise, unusual comings and goings. Gossips can turn quite innocent events into horrendous stories.

If someone dies on the premises, discuss and agree with the undertaker the most discreet way of removing the body.

Share knowledge and experience and information with businesses in your area: shops, garages, other hotels and guesthouses. Local networks are a valuable way of exchanging information about people using stolen credit cards or cheque books, likely to cause violence, suspected of handling drugs and so forth.

Social skill to admire

A well-known Premier League footballer was enjoying a lively evening with friends when one of the party returned to the room wearing a waiters' green waistcoat. Amid much hilarity, he sat down and put his feet on the table!

Paul, my brasserie manager, knew that it would only cause a confrontation if he told the guest to take his feet off the table.

"Look here," said Paul, with mock sternness, "you've no time to sit around talking to your friends. There are tables to clear and drinks to serve. Everyone else is working flat out – get your feet off that table and start helping."

Everybody fell about and a difficult situation with these excited young men was averted.

Caterer & Hotelkeeper, Reader Diaries. Denis Watkins is co-chef and senior partner of the Angel Inn, Hetton, North Yorkshire

---

Deal with problem guests

Keep on the right side of the law

- ☑ record all accidents, even minor ones, in the accident book
- ☑ report any accident or incident connected with work (including violence inflicted on a member of staff by a guest) which results in major injury and/or death to the environmental health department of your local authority
- ☑ report any violence to the police
- ☑ use only minimum force to defend yourself, your employees, your property or other guests
- ☑ you have no right to search a person or his/her property
- ☑ when someone is causing a nuisance you have the right to ask that person to leave: if he/ she refuses, call the police
- ☑ make a note of what happened, what you saw, when, where, descriptions, etc., get names and addresses of anyone who witnessed an incident
- ☑ never take risks, or put yourself in danger

if you are licensed

- ☒ do not allow anyone under 14 years of age in the bar
- ☒ do not sell or serve alcohol to under 18 year olds
- ☒ do not sell alcohol to someone buying on behalf of an under-age person
- ☒ do not permit drunken, violent, quarrelsome or disorderly conduct on the premises
- ☒ do not serve alcohol to a person who is drunk
- ☒ do not serve alcohol to a member of the police on duty

Combating fraud

- ☑ when checking other identification: always take driver's licence out of holder, and compare signature with that on card/cheque; check date of birth and sex of licence holder
- ☑ to preserve fingerprints and other forensic evidence, handle stolen credit cards, forged bank notes, valuable lost property, as little as possible and with care, e.g. by the edge – using a cloth may smudge prints (your own fingerprints can be isolated by the police)
- ☑ to mutilate and protect wanted/recovered cards: cut the bottom left hand corner from front of card, preserve intact signature strip, magnetic stripe, hologram etc.
- ☑ do not staple or pin anything to vouchers/cheques which you have retained for evidence
- ☑ keep recovered cheque/card in plastic bag

Discrimination

- ☒ do not treat a person less favourably on grounds of sex, race or disability
- ☒ do not impose a rule or condition that affects a particular racial group or sex more than others

Rights of entry

- ☑ police
- ☑ environmental health officer
- ☑ customs and excise officers
- ☑ trading standards officers
- ☑ health and safety inspector
- ☑ fire officer

Signs of drunkenness

- ▼ staggering, heavily slurred speech
- ▼ very dilated pupils, state of dress, language, disorderly

Death on the premises

- ▼ do not touch the body
- ▼ do not touch anything in the room until the police have arrived, completed their investigation and given permission
- ▼ extend comfort and assistance to any companion or relative of the deceased
- ▼ assist the police with any information which will help establish the circumstances
- ▼ offer assistance to gather the deceased's belongings: it may be appropriate to have a witness present, and to make a record of each item, to avoid ambiguity later
- ▼ for foreign nationals, inform their embassy (or check that the police will do this)
- ▼ arrange for the discreet removal of the body, so that other people are not alarmed
- ▼ arrange counselling, if necessary, for the person who first discovered the death
- ▼ ask your staff not to speak of the incident, because of the unwelcome publicity it could bring

Taking a tough line on prostitution

- ▼ challenge suspects politely, but immediately: if they say they are a friend, colleague or relative of the guest, check with the guest
- ▼ at night, explain that for safety (e.g. in the case of fire), unregistered guests are not allowed in guest rooms after a particular time
- ▼ if the guest wishes to register the suspect, point out that the bill will be for a double room at the full rate (putting both names and addresses on the bill is an additional deterrent)
- ▼ alternatively, point out that it is policy not to register additional occupants after a certain time

Please your guests

8 Profit from complaints

It is unpleasant to get a complaint, especially if you feel it is completely unjustified, or the guest is rude and bad tempered. But there is much to gain from tackling the situation in a positive, professional way.

Firstly, you have the opportunity to win over a dissatisfied guest. It's a useful rule of thumb that the satisfied complainer tells five others how well he or she was treated. Dissatisfied customers tell nine others of your failings.

Secondly, you can learn from the experience. By investigating what went wrong and why, you are likely to come up with better ways of doing things.

For example, you might identify a training need: a member of staff who could, with your help or by attending a short course perhaps, become more skilled and confident at dealing with customers.

Complaint handling: the technique

There are just three basic stages:

1 listen

2 apologise

3 take action.

The aim is to quickly diffuse the problem. Control your emotions, take charge of what's going on, and by being careful what you say and don't say, you can turn the psychology of the situation around to work in your favour.

Let the guest describe without interruption what went wrong. This way you hear the whole story before deciding on what response is appropriate. You also avoid 'winding up' the guest, making him or her more angry.

Apologies should sound sincere and be convincing. Be cautious about admitting blame. While you may earn sympathy or at least understanding from the guest for your honesty, there is a risk that you will jeopardise insurance claims or legal proceedings which may follow.

Do not make excuses or blame anyone else. Guests see this (and wouldn't you, in similar circumstances?) as trying to pass the buck. If the problem was genuinely outside your control, e.g. a power cut, or a member of staff ill, it would have been better to inform guests at the time. As the person in charge, guests expect you to minimise the inconvenience to them when such events occur.

Be polite. Thank the guest for bringing the problem to your attention. In the face of anger or rudeness, keep calm. Never argue or disagree. Proceed on the premise that guests are always right.

Dry-cleaning scam

Establishments from as far afield as Gullane in East Lothian – apparently picked at random from a hotel and restaurant guide – received an identical letter from a Miss Waters of London W8. The letter referred to a "slight accident", which occurred at an unspecified Christmas dinner and asked for recompense for an £8 dry-cleaning bill.

Simon Greenhalgh, proprietor of the 15-bedroom Mill at Harvington, was immediately suspicious as he could remember no such incident, and contacted the police. "The idea is clearly to get the hotelier to pay up on the grounds that £8 is a small amount to pay to retain the goodwill of an otherwise satisfied customer."

Angela Jameson reporting in *Caterer & Hotelkeeper*

Never offer something you cannot provide, e.g. a complimentary room at the same time next year (when you are already full). Or which is likely to be very difficult for the guest to take advantage of, e.g. upgrading on the next visit (when the guest is on a once-in-the-lifetime holiday from Australia).

How to put matters right

What, if anything, you offer the complaining guest should:

1 provide compensation in proportion to the inconvenience suffered (and, perhaps, the fuss caused)

— for example, reduced or no charge for the night on which noise from the discotheque kept the guest awake

2 have the greatest positive impact on the guest at the least real cost to you

— moving to a better room only costs you a little extra for cleaning and laundry

— reducing the room bill or offering free accommodation on a future visit has an impact on income – but again, cleaning and laundry are the only real costs

— providing a complimentary bottle of wine costs you whatever you paid for the wine – substantially less than its price on the wine list

3 where possible, provide the guest with the incentive to stay with/eat with you again, so you have a chance to excel

— a free meal or a free night's accommodation will do this, and you benefit from what the guest spends on wine and drinks, or a longer stay

— the real costs are for the food (if it is a meal), the cleaning and laundry (if it is a room).

Total satisfaction guarantee

A Surrey-based hotel group offers guests a 100% satisfaction guarantee. The scheme is promoted on posters in reception, in leaflets in the rooms, and on notepaper in conference rooms.

In the early stages of the initiative, refunds across the group's six hotels averaged £3,500 per month. By putting the focus on tackling the problems complained about, and empowering staff to do so, the level of refunds soon dropped to between £500 and £700 per month, across ten hotels.

More significant has been the impact on guests. One conference group, refunded £380 because of general dissatisfaction, were so impressed with the speed of the refund and the lack of red tape that they immediately booked three more sessions.

The operations director attends the monthly meetings held at each hotel to conduct an autopsy of refunds in the previous weeks. His presence is a reminder that the scheme is there to be applied. An unnaturally low refund rate is likely to produce a furrowed brow.

David Tarpey, *Caterer & Hotelkeeper*

Taking care of people starts with your staff

A member of staff overheard a guest attending a golf tournament say that he had forgotten to pack a suit for the evening dinner and cabaret. The employee rushed home and took a sports jacket and tie from his wardrobe to lend to the guest so that he was able to attend the dinner.

In another hotel, the receptionist offered to wash and iron clothes for an elderly guest when his wife was taken to hospital unexpectedly; the guest had packed only enough items for a weekend stay and needed clean clothes to visit her in hospital.

Both guests were full of praise for these actions and have become loyal customers. But these incidents would not have taken place if the employees themselves did not feel motivated, confident and happy.

Angie Risley, human resources director for the Whitbread Hotel Company, writing in Viewpoint, *Caterer & Hotelkeeper*

Protect yourself

Keep a record of complaints: what happened, when, who was involved, the outcome. This could be a note in your diary, or a more formal system such as a complaints book. You then have a reference should there be some un-expected development: an investigation by a Trading Standards or environmental health officer, a solicitor's letter, a letter of complaint for an incident which never occurred, a court summons.

Notes written at the time are more reliable and more useful evidence than days or weeks old memories.

Ask colleagues and staff who deal with complaints in your absence, to record similar details. If a verbal report is simpler to manage, then make your own written notes at that time.

Learn from experience

Complaints often help identify a problem that you were previously unaware of. Because it had escaped your attention, perhaps, or because you had not envisaged the particular set of circumstances occurring. Other benefits include:

1 extended repertoire of guest demands

— for example, for heating in their room in the warmest summer weather – to dry their underwear, washed overnight

2 experience of how to get the best from complaints

— what techniques worked well, e.g. upgrading to a better room

— what were less successful, e.g. offering wine with the meal, and the guests replying 'We never touch alcohol!'

3 awareness of what you can do better

— for example, stating when you take bookings that you do not accept credit cards

4 identification of failures, weaknesses and strengths in your team

— so that you can take action to help your staff do a better job

5 awareness of changing expectations of the hotel/guesthouse/farmhouse/B&B experience

— for example, that more people expect colour TV and drink-making facilities in room, en suite facilities, satellite channels, secure parking.

44

Encourage feedback

This insight can be gained with less pain when you keep closely in touch with what your guests expect and want. To encourage the communication process:

1 talk to your guests

— put them at ease so you get honest replies to your questions about the comfort of the room, what they like most (and least) about your place/other hotels they have stayed in

2 ask guests to answer a simple questionnaire (example on page 56)

— left in the room information pack, handed over on departure, or mailed later, perhaps as part of a special offer incentive

3 check during the stay that guests are satisfied

— in a convincing, sincere way, not the robot-like 'is everything satisfactory' which leaves the guest thinking that nothing would change whatever their reply

4 observe guests

— their behaviour, facial expressions and other body language

— what is said in conversation – professional eavesdropping!

5 be constantly alert for, and act on signs of dissatisfaction

— so that you can catch the problem before it becomes the reason for a complaint.

Speedy action stops the domino effect. One mistake leads to another and another, each adding to the ghastliness of the experience for the guest. Thus the wait of two minutes, becomes 10. Leave them for five minutes and they will say they have been waiting for 30. It's not that guests are unable to tell the time, but to get action they feel the need to make a point of their dissatisfaction.

A warning to read guests' comments

An entry in the guest comment book at a Stratford-upon-Avon hotel says how lovely the hotel is – but warns against staying in Room 7 "because of the droning extractor fans outside the window". An entry lower down the page remarks "Thanks for the tip, I asked to be moved out of Room 7 and they obliged."

Table Talk, *Caterer & Hotelkeeper*

The rude, the mad and the turned-ugly

Barbara Baldon has coined a new phrase for reception staff 'No reservation without confirmation', following an ugly incident.

"This American tried to check into our full hotel. Despite polite assurance that we had no reservation, he spent a good 10 minutes throwing a small fit, in front of a fairly crowded lounge, over our incompetence.

"The receptionist kept her cool, despite demands for compensation and threats to sue, and found the man somewhere else to stay.

"When I followed it through, sure enough, he had not made a reservation, merely an enquiry. Nevertheless, I wonder what all the people who witnessed the scene – who do not know it was the guest's mistake – think of us?"

Caterer & Hotelkeeper, Reader Diaries. Barbara Baldon runs the Lodge, Tal-y-Bont, Gwynedd with husband Simon

---

Thought for the day

Well respected staff pass on that goodwill to your guests. Those treated shabbily will regard the guest with apathy and nonchalance.

David Tarpey, *Caterer & Hotelkeeper*

Help your staff deal with complaints

You cannot guarantee that every complaint will come to you first. Indeed, some guests find it easier to complain to staff rather than the proprietor. So you have to make sure that anyone and everyone in the firing line knows what to do. Explain:

1 the basic complaint sequence

— listen, apologise, take action

— emphasise that colleagues should not be blamed, nor excuses made

2 how to deal with guests who are angry or upset

3 what action can be taken in response to a complaint without consulting you

— how much you empower individuals should reflect their responsibility and experience

— by taking some risks, you give staff a chance to develop themselves – more complaints will be dealt with on the spot, which guests appreciate

— an over-cautious approach, insisting that everything involves you, slows the whole process, and encourages staff to ignore complaints

— the receptionist who scuttles off at the first sign of trouble to fetch someone higher up the ladder gives a poor impression

4 how you are to be informed of complaints, and when

— as soon as possible must be the rule.

The contented chef (see right) provides an example of a staff checklist for handling complaints, which you might wish to adapt.

My guide to handling complaints

1 Keep calm. Apologise. Do not make excuses or blame anyone.

2 Establish what has happened. Do not argue with or interrupt the guest.

3 Take immediate action whenever possible, to put right what is wrong.

4 Reassure the guest: that the complaint is being dealt with, that the guest's welfare is your concern.

5 Know the limits of your authority. Refer matters which fall outside this authority promptly to the relevant person.

6 Report the incident.

9 Goodbye on the right note

The departure is the time for practicalities and courtesies. The bill has to be settled, the room key collected, the guest thanked, goodbyes said. You want the guest to leave in a positive frame of mind. Regulars to continue to return. First-time guests to become regulars. Recommendations to be made to colleagues and friends.

When breakfast is both the last meal of the guest's stay and the first meal of their day, how it is served has a big impact on the impression your guests take away.

To those people who are on edge at breakfast, untalkative, intolerant of delay, even bad humoured and grumpy, respond with tact, a subdued but friendly attitude, quiet efficiency and fast service. Keep the chatty style for those who are more relaxed.

Be prepared

Ensure the bill is accurate:

- is the charge as quoted?

- have all extras been included?

- has the deposit been deducted?

- is the guest's name spelt correctly?

Have the bill ready to hand to the guest immediately it is asked for. People anxious about a business appointment, or wanting to get on their journey, will be irritated by delays while the bill is calculated or some details checked. Nor do you want to risk leaving items off the bill, because you have had to prepare it in a hurry, and consequently overlook an extra charge for newspapers, a meal, drinks or telephone calls.

A bill which is straightforward – one-night's bed and breakfast and no extras, for example – will generally get a quick glance to confirm the total is what the guest expected. The cash or credit card is promptly handed over, or a cheque written out.

For a more complex bill, and for foreign guests who may not be familiar with our currency, allow the guest a few moments privacy to scrutinise the bill. Offer to explain anything and suggest that you return shortly.

Explain the charges

Clarity is the aim. Each item should be itemised and described, so that guests can easily check the bill is correct.

Guests who are claiming their bill as a business expense may ask for a 'VAT receipt'. If you are registered for VAT, then bills, receipts and other business stationery will carry your VAT number. But if you have recently registered and are using up your existing stock of bills, buy a rubber stamp so that you can quickly overstamp the VAT number on bills. If you are not VAT registered (because your turnover is below the threshold), explain this to the guest.

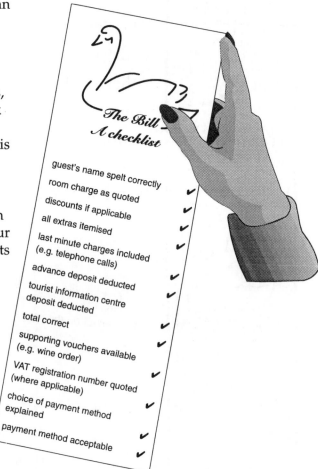

The Bill – A checklist

guest's name spelt correctly
room charge as quoted
discounts if applicable
all extras itemised
last minute charges included (e.g. telephone calls)
advance deposit deducted
tourist information centre deposit deducted
total correct
supporting vouchers available (e.g. wine order)
VAT registration number quoted (where applicable)
choice of payment method explained
payment method acceptable

Protect yourself

When accepting payment by cheque and credit card, follow carefully the advice of your bank/credit card company. With some guests you may be tempted not to carry out the usual checks, because it suggests you do not trust them. The risk you take is that payment will be refused by the bank/credit card company because:

- there are insufficient funds in the account

- or it is a stolen card or cheque book

- and you have failed to carry out the correct procedure.

Guests should understand the necessity for checks. It may help to explain that the bank or card company have issued instructions for extra precautions.

Accepting a cheque above the guarantee limit

If you do not accept credit cards, you may decide, as some shops do, to accept cheques above the guarantee limit and company cheques (for which guarantee cards cannot be obtained). To protect yourself:

1 carry out the usual checks on the guarantee card and write the number on the reverse of the cheque

— this helps establish that the card and cheque book do belong to the guest

2 obtain the full address of the account holder

— usually, you will already have this from the booking and registration records – this means you can pursue payment if the bank returns the cheque due to insufficient funds in the guest's account

3 for a guest you do not know, ask for a second form of identification

— for example, a driver's licence – so you can check that the person is who he/she claims to be, and that the address is the one given

4 if a driver's licence, passport, or other identification is not available, ask to see the guest's credit cards

— like the first point, this helps establish ownership (but is not, of course, conclusive).

Cheque plus cash

The safer method is to ask the guest to pay cash for any amount over the card limit. But what if the guest has no cash, and there is no cash machine which accepts the guest's card nearby? Or the guest offers to drive off to get cash, having already loaded luggage into the car?

Advance authorisation

It is to avoid such difficulties that many hotel groups ask for credit card details when taking the booking, and confirm method of payment at registration. Authorisation for the likely amount of the bill is obtained well before the guest's departure. If this is refused, the guest is asked to see the manager and given the option of paying cash in advance, making some other acceptable arrangement, or checking out immediately.

Accepting a credit or cheque guarantee card

- examine the card for signs of tampering or alteration
- hold the card and rub the signature strip
- watch the customer sign: hold on to the card while this is done
- match signature on the voucher or cheque with one on the card
- check signature spelling against embossed name on the card
- if card is swiped through terminal, match embossed account number against till roll
- check valid from and expiry dates
- if suspicious: do not give card back to customer, make authorisation call, or phone cheque guarantee card helpline
- if the guest challenges you on why a transaction needs authorisation, say that the bank/credit card company insist on this
- never disclose your floor limit (i.e. what you can accept without authorisation)

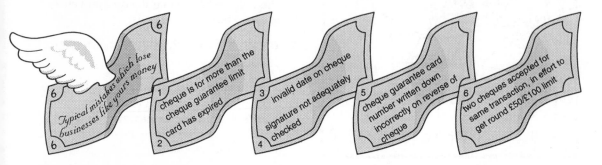

Typical mistakes which lose businesses like yours money

1 cheque is for more than the cheque guarantee limit / card has expired

2 invalid date on cheque

3 signature not adequately checked

4 cheque guarantee card number written down incorrectly on reverse of cheque

5 two cheques accepted for same transaction, in effort to get round £50/£100 limit

6

Courtesy that counts

Hopefully problems with payment will be rare or you manage to avoid them altogether. Instead, you can focus on the pleasantries. Offer to help the guest by:

- carrying the luggage: this presents an opportunity to check nothing has been left (or taken) by the guest, and to make sure you get the room key back

- calling a taxi

- giving directions for the onward journey

- checking the weather/road report

- making a booking at the destination: with a fellow member of any consortium you belong to, or through the tourist information centre network, or at a place known to or chosen by the guest

- saying a pleasant goodbye, renewing your thanks for the visit, and wishing the guest a safe journey.

Handle the irregular request

Sometimes a guest asks for the bill to be made out differently. Requests that present little or no problem include:

- separate bills for two people sharing a twin or double or members of a group, so that each person can pay the correct share and claim from expenses

- separate bills for two people sharing a twin or double, where one person can claim on expenses: discuss what split is required, or offer to put the higher portion equating to a single room on the bill which can be reclaimed

- combined bill for everyone in the group

- a tip to be added and itemised on the bill.

You have to decide at what point to say 'No' when requests move on to progressively more difficult territory:

- wines and drinks to be incorporated into the charge for dinner

- drinks, meals, etc. to be incorporated into the charge for accommodation

- a bill for two people to be described as single occupancy

- a higher sum written on the bill (needless to say, not to give you extra payment)

- a blank bill.

When considering where to draw the line, ask yourself (and perhaps the guest) what the business or organisation paying the expenses will conclude about your business if such half truths or bending of the rules are discovered.

For your own accountancy purposes, and to protect yourself should the Inland Revenue inspect your records, your copy of the bill must be accurate and honest. Bear in mind, too, that any suggestion that this copy is different from the guest's copy, creates the suspicion that you are recording a lower sum than that charged in order to reduce your income and so pay less tax.

Follow-up

Back once more to courtesies! Some guests respond to the special care and attention you have given them with a thank you letter, card or call. A definite for your Christmas card list, and perhaps for a reciprocal, handwritten note of thanks.

Words guests have written or said in appreciation make excellent endorsements for your next brochure or other marketing effort. But if you want to use the guest's name alongside the quote, get permission from the guest.

Left property

Whoever finds forgotten guest belongings should, as soon as possible, make a note of where and when the discovery was made.

A written record enables you to prove you have a system for logging left property. This helps resolve any query about ownership. It also helps protect you from claims that jewellery, passports, keys and other valuable items have been left, when you know, after another careful search, that they have not been. It is hard to argue that you have meticulous housekeeping standards, that left property is never overlooked, and always returned promptly to the owner, when you have no evidence of having done so.

What to do with left property

If, when and how you return the found property will depend on:

1 **if you can establish the ownership without doubt**

— because of where it was found, or you remember the guest wearing/using it, or the guest has told you the item is missing

— in these circumstances, there is no point in waiting for the owner to contact you

2 **if you do not know who the owner is**

— for example, were the slippers under the bed for some time before they were discovered by the cleaner? In this case, you can only wait for the item to be claimed

— how long you keep the item for, depends on its value: 6 months for valuable items, otherwise 3 months is generally considered reasonable

3 **the value of the item(s)**

— an odd sock, plain handkerchief or tube of toothpaste may not be worth keeping or returning

— whereas a child's favourite toy, a passport, keys, jewellery, heart medicine, etc. are clearly valuable to the owners

4 **urgency with which the guest needs the property back**

— from what you know of the guest or have been told

5 **where the guest can be contacted**

— you may not know the next destination of an overseas visitor or a travelling sales rep

— who the guest is: for regulars or those who spent a lot, you might be willing to pay the cost of returning the item, even if this involves registered mail for valuable items

6 **arranging how the guest will pay the cost of returning the items.**

10 Build on your success

Keep closely in touch with what your guests want, and how well you are meeting these needs in business terms. You cannot be complacent. The hospitality business which takes success for granted gets a big shock. This might happen in weeks or months if a new competitor has caught the market exactly right.

You have the strength of a distinctive product, your personal service. Focus on this, and ensure it is supported by everything else which is important to please your guests.

Looking back encourages you to analyse what accounted for improvements and disappointments compared to previous years.

Looking forward, gives you and your staff goals or targets to work towards.

Measure your success

Gut feelings and a full reservations book are reassuring, as is a healthy bank statement. But you need to have a more useful understanding of how well your business is doing in its aim of meeting guest needs. You need help too, in identifying the trends. For example, an increase in demand for single and family rooms, growing popularity of weekend breaks, guests generally staying for a shorter time, fewer visitors from France and Germany, more from North America.

Here are some simple calculations to give you this insight:

1 Room occupancy

The number of rooms occupied compared to the number available, usually expressed as a percentage.

Room occupancy can be calculated over any period you wish. Weekly or monthly and overall for the year gives a meaningful comparison with what you achieved in the past, and with general trends in your part of the country (tourist boards publish occupancy statistics regularly).

2 Bed occupancy

Calculated in the same way as room occupancy, except that it is the number of beds occupied compared to the number available.

By focusing on beds, you get a clearer picture of the pattern of occupancy of twin, double and family rooms. This is useful when you are considering your pricing policy. For example, if there is a strong demand from business guests for en suite single rooms, which you can only satisfy by letting a twin or double for single occupancy, you should be able to charge two-thirds or more of what you would for two people.

3 Average room and guest rates

Add together all the room revenue for a week/month/year and divide by the number of:

- occupied rooms

- guests.

This is a useful measure if you have a range of rates for different standards of room, times of the year, types of customer. If, for example, the achieved room rate is close to your cheapest price, you would probably conclude that you are discounting too much.

4 Average length of stay

The number of beds occupied over the month/year divided by the number of arrivals in the same period.

This is a useful way to identify changing trends, e.g. for touring holidays. The standard two-week summer holiday in a British B&B by the seaside has become a rarity.

5 Nationality of guests

The total for the year by country of origin.

How detailed you get will depend on the importance of the market to you, and whether you are considering advertising or direct mail to get more business from particular countries or regions. For example, you might separate totals for

France, Germany, the Netherlands, Republic of Ireland and other EU member countries, but combine the African countries, similarly for Asia, Australasia, North America, etc.

6 Purpose of visit

The total for the year based on what you know of guests: business, visiting friends, on holiday, for local activity events, leisure breaks, etc. as appropriate. This information helps when you are reviewing your room prices, deciding on advertising, and writing the copy for your next brochure.

THE CAMBRIAN INN
8 TWINS/DOUBLES, 2 SINGLES,
STANDARD TARIFF £20 PER PERSON IN TWIN/DOUBLE, £25 PER PERSON IN SINGLE,
10% DISCOUNT FOR GROUPS, AND STAYS OF 3 NIGHTS AND LONGER

MAY	Sunday	Monday	Tuesday	Wednesday	Thursday	Friday	Saturday
ROOMS		1 4	2 8	3 10	4 10	5 10	6 10
SLEEPERS		6	12	18	17	17	17
REVENUE		£130	£260	£370	£320	£320	£320
ARRIVALS		6	10	18	17	0	0
ROOMS	7 1	8 6	9 8	10 9	11 10	12 2	13 9
SLEEPERS	2	7	11	16	18	4	10
REVENUE	£40	£165	£245	£330	£333	£80	£240
ARRIVALS	2	5	11	8	18	4	6
ROOMS	14 4	15 7	16 8	17 10	18 8	19 8	20 8
SLEEPERS	6	11	16	16	16	16	16
REVENUE	£130	£235	£200	£340	£288	£288	£288
ARRIVALS	0	11	2	16	16	0	0
ROOMS	21 1	22 6	23 10	24 10	25 5	26 4	27 10
SLEEPERS	2	6	18	18	6	8	18
REVENUE	£36	£120	£333	£333	£140	£160	£370
ARRIVALS	2	4	18	0	6	8	10
ROOMS	28 0	29 3	30 8	31 7	TOTAL ROOMS 206	MAX 310	
SLEEPERS	0	4	10	14	TOTAL SLEEPERS 349	MAX 558	
REVENUE	0	£90	£230	£252	TOTAL REVENUE £6986		
ARRIVALS	0	4	10	6	TOTAL ARRIVALS 218		

ROOM OCCUPANCY $\frac{206 \times 100}{310} = 66\%$ BED OCCUPANCY $\frac{349 \times 100}{558} = 63\%$

AVERAGE ROOM RATE $\frac{6986}{206} = £33.90$ AVERAGE GUEST RATE $\frac{6986}{349} = £20.02$

AVERAGE LENGTH OF STAY $\frac{349}{218} = 1.6\ DAYS$

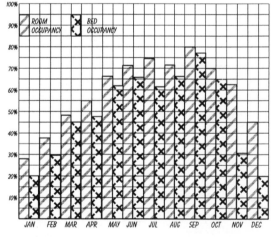

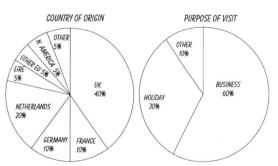

COUNTRY OF ORIGIN

PURPOSE OF VISIT

Forecasts

You can forecast the three main business measures (room and bed occupancy and achieved room rate) for the next year — by month, to be meaningful. This can only be informed guesswork, based on what you have previously achieved, your plans for targeting new business, and what you know of business trends. But the more you practise the clearer will be your understanding of the various factors which do affect your business.

Qualitative information

Conversations with a business purpose are a recurring theme in this book. Another approach is to use a simple questionnaire or guest comment card, placed in the room, or presented towards the end of the stay. You can encourage guests to complete it, by linking it to a prize draw or a discount off their next stay.

WAS OUR WELCOME FRIENDLY?
DID YOU ENJOY YOUR STAY?
WHAT DID WE DO BEST?
WHAT CAN WE DO BETTER?
WAS THE FOOD GOOD?
WAS YOUR ROOM COMFORTABLE?
HOW DID YOU... ...BOUT US?
DID YOU FIN... ...EASILY?
READY TO... ...BOOKING?

Dear Guest

We hope that you enjoyed your stay and will choose to visit us again. Our goal is to please. To help us do this, kindly complete this short questionnaire, and leave it in the box at reception before you depart.

What made you select the hotel ✔ as appropriate

previously stayed	☐
recommended by	
friends/colleagues	☐
travel agent/tourist board	☐
advertisements	☐
hotel brochure	☐
special interest break	☐
company reservation	☐
leisure facilities	☐
other *please describe*	

Satisfaction with stay	Excellent	Good	Average	Poor
welcome on arrival	☐	☐	☐	☐
service during stay	☐	☐	☐	☐
information on local attractions	☐	☐	☐	☐
breakfast	☐	☐	☐	☐
dinner	☐	☐	☐	☐
packed lunch	☐	☐	☐	☐
bar facilities	☐	☐	☐	☐
wine list	☐	☐	☐	☐
bedroom furnishings & facilities	☐	☐	☐	☐
bathroom facilities	☐	☐	☐	☐
cleanliness of:				
bedroom on arrival	☐	☐	☐	☐
bedroom during stay	☐	☐	☐	☐
public areas	☐	☐	☐	☐
overall impression	☐	☐	☐	☐

What did you enjoy most about your stay

....

....

What could have been done better or improved

....

....

Please add any other comments which would help us

....

....

Watch and learn from local competition

Do you know all the other places people can stay in your locality? What price each charges? What standards and facilities are offered? Where they are advertising?

There is no advantage in taking a timid approach to this, nor to engage in a turf war. Your competitors very likely know what your prices are. Do you not wonder about those calls asking for prices, but being rather vague about what sort of room is wanted or the date of stay? When you call 1471 to check, you find the number has been withheld. Use this tactic yourself, or if you think someone might recognise your voice, ask a friend or relative to make the calls.

Get copies of the information distributed by tourist boards. Study the advertisements in shop windows and in local newspapers. Look at the entries in hotel, B&B and other guides for your area (a little time browsing in a good bookshop will confirm which are worth buying). The small ad holiday pages in the national Sunday newspapers give a broad overview of what people are charging. Send off for information from places similar to your own. What good ideas can you get from them?

Network with other businesses

Through your local chamber of commerce, membership of the Rotarians, Women's Institute, the school parents association, sports clubs, music and theatre groups, local branches of professional and trade associations, the tourist board, etc., you can keep in close touch with what is happening to other businesses and the local economy. Information about development plans, bypasses, businesses closing, opening, expanding, contracting, tends to travel more quickly through such channels.

Being involved in all these would leave no time to run your own business, so strike a balance. And do recognise the value of a high local profile: you are more likely to be recommended when people know you.

Keep an eye on the big picture

The varying economic fortunes of UK
plc, of your own region, and of the areas
your guests come from, have a trickle
down effect on your business. A strong
pound makes the UK more expensive for
overseas visitors. High inflation puts
pressure on your costs, and makes your
customers more careful about what they
spend their money on. The state of the
housing market, of the major industries,
of those businesses which depend on
overseas investment all have an effect.

What people want from hotels and other
places they stay in is changing. When
people have got used to having a private
bathroom, and not paying a lot for it in
the mass market overseas destinations
like Majorca and the Canary Islands, they
expect one in British hotels and
guesthouses.

The minimum criteria for verification by
the tourist boards has reflected this
raising of standards. Not many years
ago, it was a wash-hand basin in all
rooms, with shaving light and point.
Now a substantial proportion of rooms
must have en suite facilities.

Plan for the future

Plan the best way to develop your
market. How can you take advantage of
the growing popularity of walking,
cycling and other outdoor pursuits? As
your regulars get too old for travel, or the
families they come to visit move
elsewhere, how can you appeal to
younger visitors who will be the regulars
of future years?

Index

Feedback your views

A series of nine *Business Guides* will focus on the issues that concern small hospitality businesses. We want this material to reflect your needs. So please take a few moments of your time to comment on the content of *Please your guests*, and the other proposed titles.

Let us have your address details and we will keep you up to date with publication developments, including the free information which industry suppliers are distributing, the audio tapes and skill checks.

Your details

Name: Mr/Mrs/Ms ....
PLEASE STATE INITIALS/FORENAME

Position: ....

Business name: ....

Type of business: Hotel/Inn/Guesthouse/B&B/Farmhouse/
Pub/Other ....
PLEASE DELETE/STATE as appropriate

Number of guest rooms: ....   Number of employees:.............

Address: ....

....

....   Postcode: ....

Tel: ....   Fax: ....

Please send me a copy on publication of the following at your special offer price† of £8.99 each plus £2 p&p per order:

❑ *Market your business*
A guide for hospitality business proprietors

❑ *The best reception*
A guide for reception, front office and reservations

❑ *Improve your business*
A guide to business analysis and planning

Special offer price

❑ Cheque enclosed for £_____

❑ Please charge £_____ to my

❑ Visa   ❑ Mastercard   ❑ Access   ❑ American Express

Account number: ....

Expiry date: ....   Signature: ....

† normal price £9.99 plus p&p

My comments on *Please your guests*

Please score on a scale of 1 to 6, 6 = excellent, 1 = poor

Ease of use ❑   Relevance of information ❑

Clarity of information ❑   Checklists ❑

Real-life examples ❑   Illustrations ❑

What I liked **most** about the book ....
....
....

What I liked **least** about the book ....
....
....

Other information on customer/guest care I would have liked to
have seen included ....
....
....

I would find these business guides:

Market your business   Useful ❑ Not useful ❑
A guide for hospitality business proprietors

The best reception   Useful ❑ Not useful ❑
A guide for reception, front office & reservations

Improve your business   Useful ❑ Not useful ❑
A guide to business analysis & planning

Build a winning team   Useful ❑ Not useful ❑
A guide to developing your own hospitality people

The best housekeeping   Useful ❑ Not useful ❑
A guide to achieving standards your guests really value

Profit from food   Useful ❑ Not useful ❑
A guide to managing the food & drink side of the business

Serve to please   Useful ❑ Not useful ❑
A guide for every hospitality team player

Deliver service excellence   Useful ❑ Not useful ❑
A guide to providing the highest standards of hospitality

About me and my business:

How many years I have run this business ....

How many years I have worked in hospitality.............................

I would be interested in sharing some of my experiences and
business success with other hospitality proprietors through your
project. Please ask one of your researchers to contact me:

Yes ❑   No ❑

Please return this form to:

Charlotte Shepheard
Macmillan Press
Houndmills
Basingstoke RG21 6XS

or fax it to: 01256 330688
*Please note, the special offer price
is only valid when your order and
payment accompanies the form.*

Further information on the series is available:
by calling the Business Guide Bookline on 01256 302945, ask for Charlotte Shepheard
by writing to Standards Development Department, Hospitality Training Foundation, International House, High Street, Ealing, London W5 5DB
by calling the Hospitality Training Helpline on 0891 44 33 22. Calls cost 50p per minute and the line is open Monday to Friday 9.30 am to 4.30 pm